$ 4·50

INTRODUCTION TO
FORTRAN

McGRAW-HILL BOOK COMPANY

New York ▪ *San Francisco* ▪ *Toronto* ▪ *London*

A PROGRAM FOR SELF-INSTRUCTION

INTRODUCTION TO

FORTRAN

S. C. PLUMB

International Business Machines Corporation

INTRODUCTION TO FORTRAN

Library of Congress Catalog Card Number 64-22199

5 6 7 8 9 10 11 12 13 14 HD 10 9 8 7

PREFACE

You are taking this course presumably to learn how a computer is programmed with FOR-TRAN. The objective of the course is to provide the knowledge and some of the skills required to *write* computer programs using the FORTRAN system; it will not transform you into a "programmer." After completing the course you will probably need some slight assistance to actually run a program on a particular computer, and considerable experience is necessary in any programming system before a high degree of proficiency can be attained. This manual will, however, provide a sound basis for attaining these goals.

A high-speed digital computer is actually nothing more than a lightning-fast calculator capable of doing arithmetic and responding to control instructions. It is not a "brain," since the programmer must "think" for the machine. Once it is instructed what to do, however, the computer will perform rapidly and accurately. This process of leading the computer by the hand through each step of the problem is the function of the "program." For instance, solving a problem on a desk calculator requires that you enter numbers in a keyboard and punch a button to cause the machine to perform an operation like addition. Thus you "program" a desk calculator one step at a time. Today's automatic electronic computers will "remember" a long list of such program steps and carry them out in their indicated order. A *program,* then, is a complete step-by-step job description for the computer. The computer interprets each step from a coded num-

v

ber; that is, the number 0300 might be a code to tell a certain computer to "add." This coded number system may be thought of as the "language" of the computer.

It is difficult and tedious to prepare programs in the computer's own language, so systems such as FORTRAN have been developed to make program writing easier. FORTRAN is a *language* itself, but it closely resembles the words and notations of the English language. Many computers have the ability, through a special intermediate program, to translate the FORTRAN language into their own number codes, so a complete computer program, or step-by-step job description, can be prepared in this simpler language and ultimately carried out by the computer. The FORTRAN *language* and its uses are the subject of this manual.

FORTRAN is introduced here at a very elementary level; no prior experience in computer programming is necessary to use this book. It will be presumed that the reader is familiar at least with high school algebra, for indeed without that, FORTRAN would be nearly useless. On the other hand, the graduate engineer will observe that the techniques demonstrated in the text are directly applicable to his, as well as simple arithmetic, problems.

There are many versions of the FORTRAN language, each of which is tailored to the features of a particular computer or computer family. The model used in this book is FORTRAN II as designed for the IBM 704/709/7090 computer family. This is the version that has been in most widespread use in recent years. The student will find that other versions differ only slightly (and that difference usually affects only a few statement types), while the important concepts and techniques are common to all versions.

The quality that entitles this book to be called self-teaching is the format of the text material. The material is presented in small units called frames, and nearly all frames require the student to check his understanding of the preceding frame or related material by responding to a short question, usually of the fill-in or true-false variety. The correct answer is immediately revealed at the start of the next frame, allowing the student to continue or stop to review if necessary. Occasionally a correct answer will instruct the student to skip review frames.

At various points the suggestion is given to solve one of the exercise problems which will demonstrate a concept or technique. A suggested solution will be given for each of these exercises. These exercises should prove quite valuable to the student, and their use is strongly recommended. Also included are two completely described programming problems, either or both of which may be programmed after completing the book. At the end of each part is a short examination covering the material within the completed segment. If the book is not used with a formal course, use of the examinations and final problems is left up to the student.

Probably the most effective way to use this book is to employ a small sheet of paper or cardboard as a mask to cover the material on the page you are reading. By sliding the mask down to, but not below, the tinted area containing the answer to a given frame, you can read the new information and the question that follows it. Then answer the question by writing it out in the book or on a separate sheet of paper. Finally, slide your mask further down the page until you have uncovered the correct answer, which can then be compared with the answer you wrote. Should your answer be incorrect, it would be well for you to review until you understand why you made the error and fully grasp the reason for the correct answer in the book, since later material builds upon your knowledge of earlier topics.

The author would like to extend his appreciation to Harvey S. Long, Thomas F. Cummings, and Richard C. Marra for their assistance and encouragement during the preparation of this book.

S. C. Plumb

CONTENTS

INTRODUCTION TO
FORTRAN

PART 1

ARITHMETIC

WITH FORTRAN

1.1 Have you read the PREFACE? [yes or no] _____

If your answer is "yes," continue with frame 1.2. If your answer is "no," better read it before continuing. You'll find it on page *v* of this text. After reading it, go to frame 1.2.

1.2 A program is written for the purpose of "leading the computer by the hand" through the steps of the problem. If the computer is going to perform arithmetic, for example, it must be told each step of the operations.

A program is a detailed description of each _____ of the solution of a problem.

> step
> You will soon learn, for example, that the FORTRAN statement
>
> $$Y = A + B + C$$
>
> represents a *program* to find the sum of the three quantities A, B, and C and to set the value of Y equal to that sum.

1.3 The statement, $Y = A + B + C$, is actually a small computer _____.

> program
> A program language such as FORTRAN is like any language; it has both vocabulary and rules of grammar and punctuation. You will learn the rules and vocabulary of FORTRAN in this course.

1.4 The FORTRAN language is particularly well adapted to mathematical problems. The way in which mathematical problems are programmed with FORTRAN closely resembles ordinary algebraic notation.

FORTRAN is particularly adapted to the programming of _____ problems.

> mathematical

1.5 The basic unit of the FORTRAN language is called a *statement*. There are 38 different types of statements, for example, in the 7090 version of FORTRAN.

The FORTRAN language is made up of 38 different types of _____.

> statements

1.6 One particular type of statement is used to tell the computer to perform mathematical computation. This statement type is called an *arithmetic formula statement*.

The arithmetic formula statement is used specifically for _____ computation.

1.7   The FORTRAN language has a method by which the computer can be told to perform basic arithmetic operations. These operations are addition, subtraction, multiplication, and division.

The example used earlier, Y = A + B + C, shows how FORTRAN tells the computer to perform the operation of _____ .

1.8   In familiar mathematical notation the basic arithmetic operations of addition, subtraction, etc., are denoted by the signs +, −, and so forth.

The − sign in ordinary notation indicates the operation of _____ .

1.9   In the FORTRAN language the operations of addition and subtraction are indicated in exactly the same way as in mathematical notation: the symbols + and − are used. The expression in FORTRAN of A + B − C indicates that the computer is to "*add* the quantities A and B and *subtract* the quantity C from that result."

The FORTRAN expression X + Y − Z + W involves the operations of _____ and _____ .

1.10   Multiplication is denoted by a slightly different, but easily remembered, symbol: the asterisk (∗). The FORTRAN expression W ∗ X indicates that the quantity W is multiplied by the quantity X.

The FORTRAN expression A ∗ X + B ∗ Y involves the operations of _____ and _____ .

1.11   FORTRAN tells the computer to *divide* quantities that are separated by the slash (/) sign. For example, the expression A/B tells the computer to "divide the quantity A by the quantity B."

3

The FORTRAN expression A * X/Z involves the operations of ___Mult___ and ___division___.

1.12   Let's see how well you understand the material presented so far. The basic operations are indicated in FORTRAN expressions by the following signs:

multiplication	___*___	subtraction	___−___
addition	___+___	division	___/___

1.13   The FORTRAN expression A + B + C − D indicates that the quantities A, B, and C are to be ___added___ and the quantity D is to be ___subtracted___ from the result.

1.14   First let's look again at the signs by which the computer is told to perform arithmetic.

+	addition	*	multiplication
−	subtraction	/	division

These signs are used in FORTRAN to tell the computer to perform _____.

1.15   Let's try another sample question. The FORTRAN expression A ∗ B/C indicates that the quantity _____ is to be multiplied by the quantity _____ and the result divided by the quantity _____.

> A, B, C
>   If you answered this question correctly, skip two frames and do Exercise 1.1. If you did not answer this question correctly, read the following paragraph and then continue with frame 1.16.

You will have to read more carefully and take more pains with the questions if you intend to continue. The material becomes much more complex in the later frames. This question is essentially the same as the previous test question: given an expression involving mathematical operations and the quantities involved, you are asked "what does the expression say?"

1.16   A person writing a program using FORTRAN or any other system is telling the computer what he wants the computer to do. In FORTRAN language, if you want the computer to add the quantities A and B you construct the expression A + B. Simple, isn't it?

If you want the computer to subtract B from X, a suitable expression in FORTRAN would be _____.

> X − B

1.17   The FORTRAN expression X ∗ Y − Z tells the computer to subtract the quantity Z from the product of X and Y.

The FORTRAN expression A ∗ S + B/T tells the computer to multiply _____ and _____ and add the result to _____ divided by _____.

> A, S, B, T
>   If you answered this question correctly, you may go on to Exercise 1.1. If you didn't get the right answer for this question, FORTRAN may be obsolete before you complete this course! Forget about world problems, money, domestic difficulties, and such trivia and *concentrate* on FORTRAN. Go back to frame 1.6 and get a running start—they don't come much easier than this chapter.

EXERCISE 1.1

Write the following expressions in FORTRAN notation (always use capital letters for the symbols in the expressions).

(a) $x + y - z$

(b) $ax + by + cz$

(c) $\dfrac{a}{b} + \dfrac{c}{d}$

(d) $a + 2b + 3c + 4d + \dfrac{5c}{2}$

$$X + Y - Z$$
$$A*X + B*Y + C*Z$$
$$A/B + C/D$$
$$A + 2*B + 3*C + 4*D + 5*C/2$$

Continue with frame 1.18.

1.18 By now you have learned how to tell the computer to perform basic arithmetic operations. You will now learn one more basic operation that can be selected by an operation sign in FORTRAN: *exponentiation*. The term *exponentiation* refers to the operation of raising a quantity to a power (squaring, cubing, etc.).

FORTRAN also permits the basic operation of _____ as well as addition, subtraction, division, and multiplication.

> exponentiation
>   (If you are familiar with squaring, cubing, etc., you may skip frame 1.19.)

1.19 The operation of exponentiation means that you multiply the number by itself the indicated number of times. For example, x^4 means x multiplied by itself 3 times, or $(x)(x)(x)(x)$.

2^{15} means the quantity 2 multiplied by itself _____ times.

> 14

1.20 The FORTRAN language has an operation sign to tell the computer to perform exponentiation: ** (double asterisk). For example, to tell the computer to raise the quantity X to the power of 2 (X squared) the sequence X ** 2 might be used.

The operation sign ** tells the computer to raise a quantity to the indicated _____ .

> power

1.21 The rule for using the exponentiation sign is simple. The quantity to the left of the sign is raised to the power indicated on the right.

In the FORTRAN expression A ** 8 the quantity _____ is raised to the power of _____ .

> A, 8

1.22 A statement may involve exponentiation along with other operations in a single statement. For example, the sequence A ** 2 + B ** 2 would tell the computer to calculate "A squared plus B squared."

The sequence A * X ** 2 − B * Y ** 3 involves the operations of _____, _____, and _____ .

1.23 The familiar notation x^2 would be interpreted as *x squared* or *x to the second power*. The computer can be told the equivalent by the notation X ** 2.

Given the formula $r = x^2 + y^3$ the equivalent can be instructed to the computer by the statement R = X_____ + Y_____ .

1.24 By now you may have noticed that FORTRAN expressions shown in the examples have consisted of *capital* letters. This convention will be continued, and *lowercase* letters will be used only for examples of ordinary formula notation, where it is to be implied that the formula is not written in FORTRAN.

Alphabetic symbols used in FORTRAN programs should be _____ letters.

1.25 The order in which the operations are carried out in a mathematical expression is most important. The algebraic expression $ab + cd$ would tell the mathematician to multiply *a* and *b*, then multiply *c* and *d*, and finally to add the two products.

It is important to know the _____ in which mathematical operations are carried out.

1.26 In the formula $x + yz$ the first operation to be performed would be _____ .

1.27   To show an example of the "hierarchy" of operations, the FORTRAN statement Y = A * B + X * Y would tell the computer to perform the two multiplication operations first, followed by the indicated addition of the products.

In the FORTRAN statement A = B * C + D the first operation performed would be _____ .

multiplication (B * C)

1.28   In the simplest form of FORTRAN expression the order of operations is determined by reading the expression from left to right.

The "hierarchy" of operations in a FORTRAN expression is dependent on scanning the expression in a _____ to _____ direction.

left, right

1.29   Reading the expression from left to right, all *exponentiation* is performed. This means *all* the indicated exponentiations are performed before any *other* types of operations are executed.

The first operation performed in a FORTRAN expression, if it is indicated, is

_____ .

exponentiation

1.30   After all the indicated exponentiations are performed, all multiplications or divisions are executed, reading again from left to right. If an expression contains both types of operation, they are still executed in the order of their appearance in the left-to-right direction.

In the FORTRAN expression F/G * H, applying the rule stated above, the operations of multiplication and division are performed in the following order: _____ , then _____ .

division, multiplication

1.31   Finally the expression is read a third time from left to right and all additions or subtractions are performed in the order in which they appear. If both types of operation are contained in an expression, they are again executed in the order of their appearance from left to right.

In the FORTRAN expression A * X − B, the *last* operation (by name) to be performed is _____ .

subtraction

1.32   The FORTRAN rule of hierarchy consists, then, of three parts:
1. All exponentiation is done first.
2. All multiplication and/or division is done second.
3. All addition and/or subtraction is done last.

The first operation performed in a FORTRAN expression would be _____ if it were indicated.

exponentiation

1.33   Each of the three groups of operations is called a "level of hierarchy." All operations on a given level must be completed before going to the next level.

The operations of multiplication and division represent a _____ of hierarchy of operations.

level

1.34   The FORTRAN statement $Y = A * X ** 2 + B * X + C$ contains all three levels of hierarchy. The computer would interpret this statement to mean:
1. Compute $X ** 2$ (exponentiation level).
2. Compute $A *$ (quantity computed in item 1) and $B * X$ (multiplication level).
3. Compute the sum of the three terms as directed (addition level) in that order.

In the statement $A = B/C + D$ the first operation to be performed would be
_____ .

division (B/C)

1.35   These rules of hierarchy are consistent with those of ordinary notation. For example, the ordinary expression $x^2 + bx + c$ would be computed by hand in the order: square x, multiply b and x, and add the three quantities. The levels of hierarchy are exactly the same as those in the FORTRAN rules. There is nothing new about these rules; you have been following them for years.

In summary, then, the FORTRAN arithmetic formula statement tells the computer to perform arithmetic operations, one at a time, thus computing an entire expression. Just as an engineer does in performing hand calculations, the operations are carried out in a specific order: exponentiation, multiplication or division, and addition or subtraction, in each case moving from left to right in the written expression until all operations at a given level of hierarchy are completed as directed.

1.36   Given the FORTRAN statement $R = A + B/C + D$, indicate in the space below which of the two following formulas this statement represents.

$$(a) \quad r = \frac{a + b}{c + d} \qquad (b) \quad r = a + \frac{b}{c} + d$$

_____

$(b) \quad r = a + \dfrac{b}{c} + d$

If your answer was (b) and therefore correct, skip two frames and do Exercise 1.2. If your answer was (a), read the following paragraph and then continue with frame 1.37.

Your answer, $r = \dfrac{a + b}{c + d}$, was incorrect. The FORTRAN statement R = A + B/C + D can be interpreted only one way according to the rules of hierarchy of operations: $r = a + \dfrac{b}{c} + d$.

1.37 To review, in a FORTRAN arithmetic formula statement all exponentiation is done first, all multiplication and/or division is performed next, and all addition and/or subtraction is done last.

Given the statement Y = C + B * X + X ** 2 the operations (by name) are carried out in the following order: _____ , _____ , and _____ .

exponentiation (X ** 2), multiplication (B * X), addition (of the three terms)

Applying these rules of hierarchy to the statement R = A + B/C + D, the interpretation is as follows: there are no exponentiations, there is one division (B/C) which is carried out first, and, finally, there are three quantities (A, D, and B/C) to be added.

1.38 Given the statement X = A/B + C indicate in the space at the right which of the two following formulas this statement represents.

$$(a) \quad x = \frac{a}{b} + c \qquad (b) \quad x = \frac{a}{b + c}$$

_____

$(a) \quad x = \dfrac{a}{b} + c$

If your answer was (a) and therefore correct, do Exercise 1.2. If your answer was (b) go back to frame 1.25 and review the material on hierarchy.

EXERCISE 1.2

In each of the following expressions show which two quantities are involved in the first operation performed.

(a) A + B + C	A	B
(b) A * B + C ** 2	C	2
(c) X * Y + A/B	X	Y
(d) A + B + C * D + X ** 3	X	3

Continue with frame 1.39.

1.39 So far you have learned to use FORTRAN to tell the computer only simple combinations of arithmetic operations. In the next few frames, you will be shown how to use parentheses to provide more flexibility in constructing mathematical expressions.

Going back to familiar formula notation, the expression $(a + b)(c + d)$ would mean "add a and b, add c and d, and multiply the two sums together." The parentheses have changed the normal order of operations.

Increased flexibility may be gained in writing mathematical expressions when _____ are used.

parentheses

1.40 FORTRAN arithmetic formula statements make use of parentheses in exactly the same way they are used in familiar mathematical notation. The FORTRAN statement $R = A * (B + C)$ tells the computer to "add the quantities B and C, then multiply this sum by A."

Indicate which of the given FORTRAN statements truly represents the formula $y = \dfrac{a}{b + c}$.

(a) $Y = A/(B + C)$ (b) $Y = A/B + C$ _____

(a) $Y = A/(B + C)$

1.41 The rules covering the use of parentheses in FORTRAN are exactly the same as those taught to the student of high school algebra. The expression $(A + B)/(C + D)$ will tell the computer to "add the quantities A and B, add the quantities C and D, *then* divide the two results."

The expression above without parentheses, $A + B/C + D$, would tell the computer to perform the operation of _____ first.

division (B/C)

1.42 Parentheses may be used freely in FORTRAN arithmetic formula statements to construct expressions of any desired degree of complexity. The use of the parentheses is pretty much governed by common sense; the instances when they are required are usually obvious.

Write an equivalent FORTRAN expression for each of the following mathematical expressions:

$a(b + c)$ _____ $ab + c$ _____

$A * (B + C),$ $A * B + C$

1.43   Parentheses are usually used only when the normal hierarchy of operations has to be altered to provide a meaningful expression. The formula $y = \dfrac{x}{a+b}$ could not be represented in a single FORTRAN expression without the use of parentheses. Y = X/A + B would certainly not be correct.

The correct FORTRAN representation of the formula $y = \dfrac{x}{a+b}$ is _____.

Y = X/(A + B)

1.44   Each use of a left parenthesis, (, must be balanced by the use of a right parenthesis,), and vice versa. For example, the expression (F + (X * Y) is not valid because of the unbalanced parentheses.

For every left parenthesis in an expression, there must be a corresponding _____ _____ .

right parenthesis

1.45   Parentheses may be used even where they are not necessarily required. Extra parentheses (as long as they are balanced in pairs) will not harm the computing efficiency.

[true or false] The expressions A * B + C * D and (A * B) + (C * D) would be considered equivalent. _____

true

1.46   Each balanced pair of parentheses sets off a group of operations which must be completely carried out before those operations outside the parentheses can be executed. For example, the expression A * (B + C + D) requires that the three quantities be added before the multiplication operation can be done.

In the example shown above, the operation of addition is carried out before the operation of multiplication; the parentheses have changed the _____ of operations.

hierarchy (or order)

1.47   Within each pair of parentheses, "exponentiation first, multiplication-division next, and addition-subtraction last" still applies. In other words each parenthesized expression is computed as if it were a complete expression subject to the usual rules of hierarchy.

In the expression X * (A ** 2 + B) the first operation to be performed by the computer would be _____.

1.48 When a group of operations within a set of parentheses is completed, that computed value usually becomes a quantity in the larger expression. For example, (A + B) * X tells the computer to "add A and B, then multiply that quantity by X."

In the expression F/(G + H) the quantity F is divided by the value of the expression _____.

To summarize, FORTRAN expressions denoting arithmetic operations are constructed in pretty much the same fashion as in ordinary notation. A set of strict rules of hierarchy must be observed, but when the expression demands it, parentheses may be used to modify the overall hierarchy of operations. The next frame contains a few examples of expressions in which parentheses *are* required.

1.49

Conventional notation	FORTRAN notation
$(a + b + c)(x + y + z)$	(A + B + C) * (X + Y + Z)
u^{n-1}	U ** (N − 1)
$\dfrac{1}{i + j + k}$	1/(I + J + K)
$[(a + b)(x + y)]^{n+1}$	((A + B) * (X + Y)) ** (N + 1)

1.50 A pair of parentheses may be completely contained within another pair, as in the example ((A + B) * C + D)/X. This would tell the computer to "add A and B, multiply this by C, add this entire result to D, and finally divide the result by X."

The innermost pair of parentheses in the example above encloses the operation of _____.

1.51 When sets of parentheses are "nested" (contained within one another), the innermost set of operations must be completely carried out before going on to the remaining parts of the overall expression.

In the expression ((A * X + B) * X + C) * X + D the innermost parentheses contain the expression _____.

1.52   The computer will interpret the expression $((A * X + B) * X + C) * X + D$ beginning in the innermost pair of parentheses, $(A * X + B)$. Once that value is computed, it becomes part of the expression in the outer parentheses, and so on.

When parenthesized expressions are "nested," the computing begins in the _____ pair of parentheses.

1.53   The general rules for parentheses are:
1. Computing begins at the innermost pair when nested.
2. Parenthesized expressions must be completely executed before other operations are executed.
3. The usual rules of hierarchy of operations apply within parentheses.
4. The result of the operations within the parentheses becomes the quantity used in the overall expression.

1.54   It should be noted that parenthesized expressions are connected to the overall expression by an operation sign in all cases. For instance, the expression $(A + B) * (C + D)$ requires that the $*$ (asterisk) sign be present to denote multiplication of the two parentheses sets. $(A + B)(C + D)$ alone is not sufficient.

Identify the correct representation below of the formula $y = \dfrac{a(b + c)}{d}$.

(a) $Y = A(B + C)/D$ (b) $Y = A * (B + C)/D$ _____

1.55   Parentheses are not needed when the natural hierarchy of operations is appropriate, but it is easy to make a slight error and end up with the wrong answer. For example, the simple expression $\dfrac{x}{yz}$ might be accidentally misrepresented by a programmer to be X/Y $*$ Z in a FORTRAN expression, while that expression actually means $\left(\dfrac{x}{y}\right)(z)$ to the computer owing to the left-to-right nature of the hierarchy rule.

By adding parentheses the FORTRAN expression X/Y $*$ Z can be made to truly represent the expression $\dfrac{x}{yz}$ as follows: _____.

1.56   It is a good idea to use parentheses wherever any doubt exists, as the preceding example showed. Excess parentheses will not harm a FORTRAN statement, but the absence of parentheses when they are needed can be disastrous!

The FORTRAN expression A/B/C means (a) $\dfrac{a}{bc}$ or (b) $\dfrac{a}{b/c}$ (select one).

(a) $\dfrac{a}{bc}$

1.57 You have seen that the FORTRAN expression A/B/C is interpreted as if it were parenthesized as ((A/B)/C) due to the left-to-right nature of the hierarchy rule. This demonstrates that, even without parentheses, there is only one way to interpret any FORTRAN expression within the rules.

Show how the basic expression A/B/C must be parenthesized to represent the formula $\dfrac{a}{b/c}$. _____

A/(B/C)

1.58 Write a FORTRAN expression to represent the formula $\dfrac{(x)(y)}{(w)(z)}$. _____ (Use corresponding capital letters as symbols.)

X * Y/(W * Z) (NOTE: parentheses are necessary.)
Other possible answers are X/W * Y/Z or (X * Y)/(W * Z) or similar combinations.
If your answer agrees with any of the above, skip to page 16 and do Exercise 1.3. If you did not have the correct answer, continue with the next frame.

1.59 Perhaps you forgot some necessary parentheses. Given the expression $\dfrac{xy}{wz}$ to construct an equivalent FORTRAN expression, the most obvious approach might be to construct the numerator X * Y, the denominator W * Z, and then place a division sign between them: X * Y/W * Z.

1.60 This answer, X * Y/W * Z, is incorrect because the computer interprets this as follows (left to right): multiply X and Y, divide that result by W, then multiply that entire result by Z, which is incorrect. This answer is equivalent to $\left(\dfrac{xy}{w}\right)(z)$, not $\dfrac{xy}{wz}$. In order to make sure that the computer multiplies Z * W before division takes place, a pair of parentheses should be placed around the denominator, as in X * Y/(W * Z), which is a correct answer.

1.61   Construct a FORTRAN expression equivalent to $\dfrac{a + (b/c)}{xy}$ using corresponding capital letter symbols. _____

(A + B/C)/(X * Y)

   If your answer agrees with the one shown above, do Exercise 1.3. If your answer is incorrect, return to frame 1.39 and review the material on parentheses.

EXERCISE 1.3

In each of the following expressions show which two quantities are involved in the first operation performed.

(a)	(A + B) + (C + D)	A	B
(b)	(A + B + X * Y) * Z	X	Y
(c)	X * (Y + Z)	Y	Z
(d)	A/B/(C * D ** 2)	D	2

1.62   Up to this point we have not been concerned with the quantities involved in the arithmetic operations. We have simply used alphabetic symbols to represent these quantities, as in the example, $Y = A + B + C$. In this arithmetic formula statement, A, B, C, and Y represent the *quantities* or numbers used in the arithmetic operations.

_____ symbols may be used to represent quantities in an arithmetic formula statement.

Alphabetic

1.63   You will now be shown that the *quantities* specified in an arithmetic formula statement may be represented in two ways: as *constants* and *variables*. These terms will be defined and illustrated in the next few frames.

   There are two ways to represent the _____ specified in an arithmetic formula statement.

quantities

1.64   One way to specify a quantity in a FORTRAN arithmetic formula statement is to represent the quantity by the actual number itself. This type of specification is called a *constant*. For example,

$$Y = 2. + 1.$$

tells the computer to add the constants *two* and *one*.

A *number* used to specify a quantity (in an arithmetic formula statement) is called a _____ .

1.65 In general, a constant is a known quantity in a mathematical expression. For example, the formula for the approximate area of a circle is A = 3.14159 r^2 in which the quantities 3.14159 (pi) and the exponent 2 are known values of constants.

The constants in the formula $0.5gt^2$ are _____ and _____ .

1.66 In a FORTRAN expression, all constants are represented by the number itself. An arithmetic formula statement to find the area of a circle, for example, might be A = 3.14159 * R ** 2.

The FORTRAN constants in the expression above are _____ and _____ .

1.67 Any quantity in a FORTRAN expression which is known at the time the expression is written can be expressed as a *constant*. The desired value is simply written into the expression as the number itself.

Write a FORTRAN expression to represent the expression $3.5x^2 - 2.9x - 0.5$ using capital letters for the symbols. _____

1.68 The other method of representing quantities in a FORTRAN expression is through the use of *variables*. The symbol X in the answer shown above is a variable.

Quantities may be represented in a FORTRAN expression as either constants or _____ .

1.69 A *variable* is defined as a symbol in a FORTRAN expression which represents a quantity whose value is specified elsewhere in the program, usually by some previous statement.

In the expression A * X ** 2 + B, the symbols A, X, and B are called _____ .

1.70   The numeric value associated with a variable is referred to by the use of its *variable name* in an expression. For example, in the expression A + B the computer is told to "add the quantity whose name is A to the quantity whose name is B."

The value of a variable is obtained for use in an expression by the reference to its _____ .

name (or symbol)

1.71   The value of a variable may change repeatedly during the execution of a program. The value of a constant, as the term implies, may not be altered.

In the expression 3.0 * X the value of the variable named _____ is multiplied by the constant _____ .

X, 3.0

1.72   The variable name acts as the symbolic "handle" of a number whose value is to be used in an expression. Use of this symbolic name permits the programmer to write the expression without knowing the exact value to be used.

In the FORTRAN expression X + Y − Z, the variables _____ , _____ , and _____ represent numbers which are to be added and subtracted as the expression directs.

X, Y, Z

1.73   When a variable is used in a FORTRAN expression, it is assumed that the programmer will have defined its value in some other part of the program.

The FORTRAN expression A * B + X/Y uses previously defined _____ in place of the symbols when the expression is computed.

values (or numbers)

1.74   At the time a program is written, a variable name is invented for each such unknown quantity and that name is written in the FORTRAN mathematical expression in place of the number it represents.

In the FORTRAN expression R ** 20 − S * T, the *first* operation to be executed is raising the predefined value of the variable _____ to the power of _____ .

R, 20

1.75   FORTRAN has rules for naming the variables used in an expression. In 7090 FORTRAN, for example, a variable may have from 1 to 6 alphabetic or numeric characters in its name. Other versions of the FORTRAN language have similar rules for the naming of variables.

A variable name may have from _____ to _____ alphabetic or numeric characters.

1.76   Although a variable may have more than one character in its name and may also use numeric characters, the *first* character in any variable name must be *alphabetic*. Thus X1 is a legitimate variable, but 1X is not.

The first character in any variable name must be _____ .

1.77   Being able to use more than one character in a variable name gives a great deal of added flexibility in the construction of expressions. The Ohm's law formula could be written in FORTRAN as Y = A * B, but the symbols become more significant if the formula is written VOLTS = CURRNT * RESIST.

1.78   A list of typical variable names is shown below:

X	DELTA
ANSWER	X12Y24
PI	NUMBER
X1	Y2

The variable name CURRENT is not a legitimate variable name because it contains more than _____ characters.

1.79   FORTRAN can tell the computer to perform two different kinds of arithmetic: *floating-point* and *fixed-point* (integer) arithmetic. These two types of arithmetic are called *modes*.

The computer's two forms of arithmetic—fixed-point and floating-point—are called _____ of arithmetic.

1.80   The *floating-point* mode of arithmetic should be used for nearly all computation. This mode automatically takes care of placing the decimal point in the results in the correct position.

Nearly all computation should be performed in the computer's _____ mode.

1.81 The *fixed-point* mode of arithmetic makes use of the integer, or whole number, and, as such, is useful only as a counter and in similar operations.

The fixed-point mode of arithmetic is used for counting and other operations involving _____ numbers.

1.82 Since most computer work involves other than whole number quantities, the floating-point mode is used almost exclusively for ordinary computation. In the floating-point mode, almost any number (including fractional quantities) may be handled automatically by the computer.

Numbers which contain fractional parts *must* be handled in the _____ _____ mode.

1.83 The programmer indicates the mode of arithmetic that the computer is to use by the nature of the variables and constants used in the FORTRAN expressions. Thus, constants and variables each have a definite mode.

The mode of the arithmetic performed is determined by the mode of the _____ and _____ written in the FORTRAN expressions.

1.84 An expression containing floating-point constants and variables will be computed using floating-point arithmetic procedures; similarly, expressions containing fixed-point constants and variables will be executed in the fixed-point mode.

1.85 A constant in the floating-point mode is identified by the presence of a *decimal point*. All constants that have decimal points are floating-point expressions.

[true or false] All the constants in the list below are floating-point constants.

_____

3.1415926	0.00000000001
5280.0	10000000000000.
11001	32.174

1.86   Fixed-point constants are numbers that do not contain a decimal point. Since all fixed-point numbers are integer or whole number quantities, no decimal point would be needed and this provides a convenient means of distinguishing between the modes of constants.

[true or false] 32678 is an example of a fixed-point constant. _____

> true

1.87   A floating-point number may be a whole number, but as a constant it must still contain a decimal point.

Write the quantity "one million" as a floating-point constant. _____

> 1000000.
>   (Must include the decimal point.)

1.88   Incidentally, commas are not permitted in constants of either mode; that is, the constant 1,000,000 is not permitted as a FORTRAN constant.

The presence of a decimal point in a constant identifies it as a _____
_____ number.

> floating-point

1.89   Zeroes after a decimal point are not necessary for a floating-point whole number. For example, the constants 1.0 and 1. are identical as FORTRAN constants.

[true or false] The constant 5,280.0 is a legitimate floating-point constant.

_____

> false
>   (Comma not permitted.)

1.90   The quantities represented by variable names must also be identified with one of the two modes. The mode of a variable is determined by the *first* letter in the variable name.

123.321 is an example of a _____-point constant.

> floating

1.91   Let's review the rule for naming a variable. A variable name may have from *one* to *six* alphabetic or numeric characters, and the first character must be alphabetic.

[true or false] All the variable names in the list below are legitimate. _____

X   A12345

X1Y2   DELTAX

1.92   The mode of a variable is determined by the first character in its name. If the variable name begins with any of the letters I, J, K, L, M, or N, it is a *fixed-point* variable; if it begins with any other letter, it is a *floating-point* variable.

The mode of a variable depends on the _____ character in the variable name.

1.93   A fixed-point variable name begins with the letter I, J, K, L, M, or N. For example, I, N, JOB, LETTER, NUMBER, KAPPA, etc., are names of *fixed-point* variables.

The fixed-point variable in the list below is _____ .

FRANK

JOE

HENRY

1.94   A floating-point variable name begins with any alphabetic character except I, J, K, L, M, or N. Under this rule, the names X, Y, DELTA, YPRIME, AIDOT, etc., are all legitimate floating-point variables.

The name FIXED is a _____-point variable name.

1.95   Remember, it is only the *first* character in a variable that is important to the mode. The letters I, J, K, L, M, and N may be used in a floating-point variable name as long as they are not the first character.

[true or false] The variable name XIJKLM is a floating-point variable. _____

1.96   Variable names are often invented to coincide with a meaningful word describing the quantity in the expression. You must be careful to avoid accidentally using the letters I, J, K, L, M, or N as the first character in an intended floating-point variable.

[true or false] The FORTRAN statement FORCE = MASS * ACCEL contains only floating-point variables. _____

1.97 Sometimes a desirable name for a floating-point variable, such as in the preceding example, begins with one of the forbidden letters. In this case an extra letter is often added to the front of the name to make it a legal floating-point variable. For example, MASS might be renamed as AMASS or XMASS, etc.

By adding a letter X in the appropriate place, the statement FORCE = MASS * ACCEL can be made to contain only floating-point quantities as follows: _____ .

FORCE = XMASS * ACCEL

1.98 To review for a moment, you now know that quantities or numbers can be represented in a FORTRAN expression as their exact value (constants) or as a symbolic name (variables), and that the arithmetic indicated in an expression is performed in one of two modes. The mode of the arithmetic is determined by the mode of the variables and constants in the expression. The mode of a constant is defined by the presence or absence of a decimal point; the mode of a variable depends on the first letter.

EXERCISE 1.4

Identify the mode of each of the variables and constants below:

(a) XSUBI _floating pt var_
(b) 0.333333 _floating pt cont_
(c) JAMES _fixed pt var_
(d) 5280. _floating pt cont_
(e) KOUNT _fixed pt var_
(f) 5280 _fixed pt cont_
(g) MASS _fixed pt var_
(h) OPERND _floating pt var_
(i) B58 _floating pt var_
(j) INSIDE _fixed pt var_

1.99 In FORTRAN terminology, an *expression* is defined as *any* combination of constants, variables, and operation signs. For example, A * X ** 2 + B * X − C is called an "expression" or more exactly a "FORTRAN expression."

$F + G - Z$ is a combination of variables and operation signs, and, as such, falls within the definition of a FORTRAN _____ .

1.100 By the definition in the preceding frame, a single constant or single variable may also be considered an "expression." Even a variable or constant preceded by a minus sign is a legitimate expression.

[true or false] All the examples in the list below are legitimate expressions.

_____

A * X + B   X ** 2 − 4.0

FRAME − FRAME   − FRAME

1.101 The "expression" is FORTRAN's method of telling the computer exactly what arithmetic operations you wish to have executed and exactly which quantities to use. The expression A + B says "add the quantities A and B," while the expression − X says "find the negative of the quantity called X."

If the numeric quantity −2.5 is represented by the name ROOT, the expression − ROOT will have a computed value of _____ .

1.102 An expression defines a series of related mathematical operations which the computer is to carry out. Therefore, all quantities in an expression must be of the same mode. (There are three special cases which are exceptions to this rule and will be explained later.)

[true or false] The expression X + 1 is illegal because of mixed modes.

_____

1.103 The expression X + 1 is indeed illegal because of mixed modes; the variable X is a floating-point quantity, and the constant 1 is a fixed-point number. All the quantities in an expression must be of the same mode.

The illegal expression X + 1 can be corrected and written in floating-point mode as _____ .

1.104 Fixed-point and floating-point numbers look quite different to the computer. It would be impossible to perform normal operations with numbers of opposite modes. Therefore, it is important that you take extreme care to keep the expressions consistent in mode.

[true or false] The expression $2 * I - 3. * X$ is a legitimate expression. _____

false
   (Opposite modes.)

1.105 One of the exceptions to the mixed-mode rule is exponentiation. Specifically, *floating-point* quantities may be raised to *fixed-point* powers, although the reverse is not true. Thus, $X ** 2$ or $Z ** N$ are quite all right; $J ** 2.$ is illegal.

One of the exceptions to the rule of consistent modes is the operation of _____ .

exponentiation

1.106 Incidentally, exponents themselves may be expressions. That is, an exponent may be a constant, a variable, or an expression involving *more* than one quantity. The latter case, however, will always require an extra set of parentheses. For example, $X ** 2$, $X ** N$, or $X ** (2 * N - 1)$ are all legitimate.

Using a fixed-point expression for an exponent, write an expression to compute the formula u^{2i+j}. _____

U ** (2 * I + J)

1.107 While we're talking about exponents, it should be noted that wherever possible FORTRAN exponents should be fixed-point in mode, regardless of the mode of the quantity being raised to the indicated power. A floating-point exponent should only be used when a fractional or mixed-number exponent is necessary.

The expressions $X ** 2.0$ and $X ** 2$ are exactly equivalent mathematically, but _____ (choose one) is preferred.

X ** 2
   (Fixed-point exponent.)

1.108 An example of the use of a floating-point exponent would be the computation of a fourth root which might be expressed as $X ** 0.25$. The need for floating-point exponents seldom arises so a good rule of thumb would be to avoid their use and stick to fixed-point exponents for either mode of expression.

When the ** notation is used for exponentiation and whole-number quantities are used for exponents, the mode of the exponent should be _____-point.

1.109 So far, reference has been made to the FORTRAN arithmetic formula statement without actually defining it. An arithmetic formula statement consists of a variable name, followed by an equals sign, followed in turn by any desired expression.

The variable name and expression of an arithmetic formula statement are separated by an _____ sign.

1.110 All arithmetic formula statements conform to this format. The computer executes the following steps for any arithmetic formula statement: "compute the complete expression on the right of the equals sign and assign that computed value to the variable whose name appears on the left of the equals sign."

In the arithmetic formula statement $A = B * C/D$ the *last* step the computer does is to assign the expression's computed value to the variable _____ .

1.111 An expression, remember, is any desired combination of variables, constants, and operation signs describing a series of arithmetic operations. The arithmetic formula statement always has some expression on the right of the equals sign.

In executing an arithmetic formula statement, the computer obtains the computed value of the _____ first.

1.112 Once the value of the expression on the right of the equals sign has been obtained by the computer, that quantity becomes the value of the variable on the left of the equals sign. For example, if the variable A has a value of 5.2 at the time the statement $Y = A + 1.$ is executed, the variable Y will end up with the value 6.2.

Assuming the same value for A, the value of X after executing the statement $X = 2. * A$ is _____ .

1.113 The format of the arithmetic formula statement is limited because only a *single variable* may appear on the left of the equals sign. The programmer may construct almost any expression on the right of the equals sign, however.

[true or false] The statement A + B = X * Y is an arithmetic formula statement.
_____

false
(Only a single variable is permitted on the left of the equals sign.)

1.114 You were told a while back that there were several ways of defining the value of a variable; the arithmetic formula is one such method.

After executing the statement Y = −0.55 the value of the variable Y will be _____ .

−0.55

1.115 After executing an arithmetic formula statement the variable on the left of the equals sign will have the value of the computed expression, regardless of what the previous value of that variable may have been.

If the statements A = 2. and B = A ** 2 were executed in that order, the value of B would be _____ .

4.

1.116 To review, you have been shown that an arithmetic formula statement consists of a variable, an equals sign, and some expression. The expression may be a single constant, a single variable, or a complex combination of operations. The statement is executed in two steps: (1) the expression, however complicated, is computed and, (2) that computed value becomes the value of the variable on the left of the equals sign.

Assume the following statements are executed in the order written. After execution by the computer, show the values of the variables A, B, C, X, and Y.

A = 2.0	A	_____
B = −3.0	B	_____
C = −2.0	C	_____
X = 2.0	X	_____
Y = A * X ** 2 + B * X + C	Y	_____

A 2.0,   B −3.0,   C −2.0,   X 2.0,   Y 0.0
If your answers were correct, skip to page 29 and do Exercise 1.5. If your answers did not agree with the ones shown above, continue with frame 1.117.

1.117 The previous frame shows a series of arithmetic formula statements to be executed in the order written. The first statement, A = 2.0, tells the computer to assign the value of the expression (2.0) to the variable called A.

The value of A after executing that statement must be ＿＿＿＿＿＿.

> 2.0

1.118 Similarly, the next three statements, B = −3.0, C = −2.0, and X = 2.0, replace the former values of B, C, and X with the corresponding expression values.

The value of X after completing the statements above must be ＿＿＿＿＿＿.

> 2.0

1.119 The last statement, Y = A * X ** 2 + B * X + C, tells the computer to perform the indicated operations using the most recently defined value of each variable.

[true or false] After the statement X = 2.0 is executed, the variable X will have the value of 2.0 regardless of its previous value.

> true

1.120 The expression in the final statement was A * X ** 2 + B * X + C. According to the rules of hierarchy, this means compute X ** 2 (4.0), multiply this by A (2.0 times 4.0), multiply B * X (2.0 times −3.0 equals −6.0), and add the indicated quantities (8.0 + (−6.0) + (−2.0) = 0.0).

The computed value of the expression shown above is ＿＿＿＿＿＿.

> 0.0

1.121 The computed value in the preceding frame then becomes the value of the variable on the left of the equals sign. In this case, the variable name is Y.

[true or false] The expression on the right of the equals sign in any arithmetic formula statement must be completely computed before any value is assigned to the variable on the left. ＿＿＿＿＿＿

> true

1.122 Given the following statements to be executed in the order written,

$$X = 3.0$$
$$Y = 2.0$$
$$A = X ** 2 - Y ** 3$$

show the values of the variables X _____ , Y _____ , and A _____
after execution of all three statements.

If your answers agree with the ones shown, do Exercise 1.5. If your
answers disagree with the correct answers, go back to page 26, frame 1.109,
and review the material on arithmetic formula statements.

EXERCISE 1.5

Identify each of the following expressions as fixed-point, floating-point,
or mixed modes.

    (a)   (A + B) * (A − B)   *floating pt.*

    (b)   (I * J + N * K) * P   *mixed*

    (c)   XI * R   *floating.*

    (d)   JOE + JIM + HENRY   *mixed*

    (e)   JEAN + JANE + LOIS − KATHY   *fixed*

1.123   When an arithmetic formula statement is executed, the most recently
defined values of the indicated variables are used. Until *some* value has been
defined for a variable, there is no way of assuring yourself that *for all computers*
the value of the variable will be zero.

Write an arithmetic formula statement that will set the value of a variable
named G equal to the value 32.174. _____

1.124   This method of setting the values of variables equal to a constant
is one way of defining the initial value of some variables. Another way to define
initial values is to tell the computer to "read" numbers from some input medium
which you will learn about later in the course.

[true or false] Until a value has been defined for any variable, its value for all
machines is zero. _____

1.125   The execution of an arithmetic formula statement changes the value of
only *one* variable—the one to the left of the equals sign. All variables used on the
right of the equals sign remain the same value.

[true or false] Before the statement $S = S0 + Y0 * T + .5 * G * T ** 2$ can be successfully executed (with the correct answer), the variables S0, Y0, G, and T must have their values defined. _____

true

1.126 Remember, the expression on the right of the equals sign must contain quantities of only one mode (except for fixed-point exponents in floating-point expressions). When this restriction is not observed, an illegal "mixed expression" results.

Identify (by letter) the single mixed expression in the examples shown below. _____

(a) $(A + B) ** (N - 2 * J)$
(b) $I * J ** LUMP$
(c) $FIX * FLOAT ** K - 1$

(c) $FIX * FLOAT ** K - 1$

1.127 The mode of the expression is determined by the mode of the quantities involved. If the expression contains floating-point variables and constants (even if fixed-point exponents are used), it is considered a floating-point expression.

The expression $F ** (I + J - K * M - 1)$ is a _____-point expression.

floating

1.128 If an expression contains fixed-point variables and constants it is considered to be a fixed-point expression. Remember, fixed-point arithmetic involves *only* integer or whole-number quantities. The results, therefore, are also fixed-point *integer* quantities.

The expression $INDEX ** (NUMBER - 1)$ is a _____-point expression.

fixed

1.129 The fact that fixed-point arithmetic produces fixed-point or integer results may cause errors under a certain condition. Although addition, subtraction, and multiplication of integers can produce only integer values, the division of integers may result in numbers with fractional parts.

The result of dividing 5 by 2 is _____ in normal arithmetic.

$2\frac{1}{2}$

1.130 Fixed-point arithmetic can permit only integer results, even for division operations. If a division operation results in a value with fractional parts, the fraction is dropped, or "truncated," *without* rounding to the nearest whole number. Thus, in the computer's fixed-point arithmetic, 5/2 comes out as 2.

If the result of a fixed-point division were 1.9999999 (true result), the computer would consider the result to be _____ .

> **1**
>
> (Dropping the fractional part without rounding.)

1.131   The reason for warning you of this characteristic is to help you avoid harmless-looking situations that could produce incorrect results. For example, assume I, J, and K have the values 5, 2, and 4, respectively. The expression I/J * K might appear to compute

$$\frac{(5)(4)}{2} = 10$$

but due to the hierarchy rules the result is (5/2)(4) which equals 8 in fixed-point arithmetic.

The expression X ** (1/2) is not equivalent to X ** .5, because the exponent in the first example (in fixed-point terms) is _____ (number).

> zero (0)

1.132   In review, then, arithmetic formula statements are used in FORTRAN programs to evaluate an expression (anywhere from a single quantity to a complicated series of operations), and assign that value to an indicated variable. These statements may be used in a program to initialize variables, change the values of variables, or provide the steps to solve a mathematical formula. Most actual arithmetic is done in the floating-point mode while special purpose operations such as exponents and counting may use the fixed-point mode.

EXERCISE 1.6

Write the following common formulas as FORTRAN arithmetic formula statements. Be careful of mode.

(a) $f = ma$

(b) $v = \frac{4}{3}\pi r^3$ ($\pi = 3.1415926$)

(c) $y = ax^2 + bx + c$

(d) $s = s_0 + v_0 t + \frac{1}{2}gt^2$

> F = XM * A
> V = 4/3. * 3.1415926 * R ** 3.
> Y = A * X ** 2 + B * X + C
> S = SO + VO * T + 1./2. * G * T ** 2
>   or 0.5

1.133   An arithmetic formula statement is executed in two distinct steps. That is, the expression is computed with no regard to the variable on the *left* of the equals sign. Thus, FORTRAN rules permit quantities on *opposite* sides of the equals sign to be of opposite modes.

31

1.134 An arithmetic formula such as A = I * J − K is perfectly legitimate under FORTRAN rules. The statement is executed as follows: (1) compute the fixed-point expression (in fixed-point arithmetic steps); (2) *convert* the result to floating-point form (the computer can be told to change the form of the number); and (3) assign this floating-point value to the variable A.

[true or false] The variable on the left of the equals sign in an arithmetic formula statement need not be of the same mode as the expression on the right.

_____

true

1.135 The general rule describing the execution of an arithmetic formula statement becomes: "the expression is completely computed in its basic mode and that value is assigned to the variable on the left of the equals sign, converting its mode if indicated."

Under this rule, the value of the variable K after executing the statement K = 1.9999999 will be _____ .

1
    (The value 1.9999999 is converted to fixed-point.)

1.136 For example, you might wish to initialize the variable X with a value of one and the statement X = 1 is perfectly legal. This is not good programming, however, since the computer must go through the steps of converting the constant (1) to a floating-point form (1.), thus wasting time.

To avoid wasting time in setting the value of X to a value of one, the statement should be _____ .

X = 1.0

1.137 This feature of changing modes is useful under special conditions, but care should be taken to see that this doesn't happen when it is not intended. This would happen when a variable is accidentally assigned a fixed-point name when floating-point is intended.

[true or false] The statement I = V/R is legitimate but will produce a fixed-point result for the variable I. _____

true

1.138 Remember, when floating-point quantities are converted to fixed-point mode form, they lose their fractional parts without rounding. A result that was intended to be 3.8759 might accidentally end up as 3 if the mode were accidentally changed from floating to fixed by an arithmetic formula statement.

Care must be taken in assigning variable names (with respect to the first letters of the name) so that the result does not end up in the wrong _____ .

1.139 Naturally, if you accidentally assign the wrong mode in a variable name that is used in an *expression,* it will not be permitted (mixed expression). If the variable is on the left of the equals sign, however, it will be allowed as a legitimate statement and incorrect answers may result.

1.140 Since an arithmetic formula statement is executed in two phases (compute the expression and assign the value to the variable on the left of the equals sign), the expression on the right may contain the same variable name that appears on the left of the equals sign.

[true or false] By the above rule the statement I = I + 1 is legal. _____

1.141 In this sense the arithmetic formula statement is not an *equation* and the equals sign really means "is replaced by" rather than "equals." Thus the statement I = I + 1 is perfectly legal and means to the computer that "the quantity 1 is added to the quantity called I, and that result replaces the old value of the quantity called I."

1.142 This form of statement is very common in programming. In the statement I = I + 1, the quantity I can be considered a counter which has 1 added to it each time this statement or a similar one is executed. The value of I may indicate how many times the statement has been executed, for example.

If the variable N has a value of 63 before executing the statement N = N − 3, it will have a value of _____ after the statement is executed.

1.143 The examples in this frame and the following frame involve very simple steps intended to demonstrate exactly what goes on when an arithmetic formula statement is executed.

Statement: A = 3./2.

Computer divides the constant 3. by the constant 2. and places the result (1.5) in A.

1.144 Statement: A = 3/2

Computer divides (fixed-point) the constant 3 by the constant 2; the result is 1 (truncated), which is converted to floating-point (1.0) and placed in A.

1.145 Up to now variables and their associated variable names have been defined as a way of referring to a single quantity by means of a symbolic label. In the FORTRAN language a variable may represent a list or array of numbers instead of a single quantity.

1.146 When a single variable name is to represent a list of numbers there must be a means of referring to a specific member of that list. FORTRAN accomplishes this through the use of *subscripts*.

1.147 A "subscript" in FORTRAN notation consists of a constant or variable (or limited expression) attached to a variable name and contained in parentheses. X(I), NAME(20), and ARRAY(N + 1) are examples of variables with subscripts, and as such are called "subscripted variables."

Variables which refer to a list or array of numbers are called _____ variables.

---

subscripted

1.148 The subscript serves to indicate exactly which number in the list is being referenced. For example, the subscripted variable X(25) refers to the 25th number in the list called X. The use of the form X(I) will refer to "Ith" number in the X list, depending on the value of the variable I.

The expression A(7) * B will tell the computer to multiply the _____th number in the A array by the quantity B.

---

seven

1.149 Thus numbers which can be meaningfully referenced in the list form can be referred to in a program by the subscripted variable form. A variable name followed by a pair of parentheses containing a subscript will refer to a particular quantity in a list, the order in the list being determined by the value of the subscript.

If the variable I has a value of 3, the subscripted variable G(2 * I) refers to the _____th number in the G array.

---

six

1.150 The list of numbers which may be referenced by a single variable name is of a predetermined length. A special statement covered by a later part is used to declare all variables whose names will be used to represent such lists as well as indicating the exact length of each list.

A subscript indicates a particular member of a list according to the numerical _____ of the subscript.

1.151   Since all lists have certain predetermined lengths, care must be taken to ensure that no subscript value exceeds the length of the list to which it refers. For example, a subscript which refers to a list called X consisting of 20 numbers should not exceed a value of 20.

A subscript used with the variable X described above may have a value between _____ and _____ .

1.152   A *subscripted variable* may be either fixed-point or floating-point mode, but all *subscripts* are in the fixed-point mode. This is the second exception to the mixed expression rule: floating-point variable names may (in fact, must) have a fixed-point subscript if subscript notation is used.

[true or false] The subscripted variable Y(T) is not a legal use of subscript notations. _____

1.153   To review, expressions of either mode may contain variables with subscripts attached which refer to a particular *single* quantity in a list; the variable(s) must be consistent with the mode of the expression but regardless of the expression's mode the subscript must be fixed-point; a particular subscripted variable refers to a specific number in the list by order according to the value of the subscript.

1.154   Most subscripts are either constants or variables, and all are in the fixed-point mode. That is, to refer to the 101st number in an array, the subscript 101 is used, or to refer to the Nth number in a list the subscript N is used with its value computed elsewhere. Certain limited expressions are permitted as subscripts also, and their rules are listed in the following frame.

1.155

Permitted expression form	Example
Variable plus or minus a *constant*	X(N − 1) or X(N + 1)
Constant multiplied by a *variable*	X(2 * N)
Constant multiplied by a *variable* plus or minus a *constant*	X(2 * N + 5) or X(2 * N − 1)

(1620 FORTRAN is somewhat more limited; consult the appropriate manual.)

EXERCISE 1.7

Identify the correct examples of subscripting shown below with a + sign and the incorrect ones with a − sign.

(a) ARRAY (LIST)   −
(b) NAME (M * N)   −
(c) A (2 * I + 1)   +
(d) ANSWER (K − 25)   +
(e) BLOCK (I + J)   −

1.156   A computer, like a desk calculator, can hold a certain size of number as a maximum. In the 7090 the size of numbers is $\pm 10^{38}$ in the floating-point mode, and $\pm 2^{17}$ in the fixed-point mode.

In floating-point calculations on the 7090 no quantity can exceed a value of + _____ .

10^{38}

1.157   The restriction on the size of numbers applies to both variables and constants. The value of any floating-point variable or constant must be within the range of $\pm 10^{38}$ and all fixed-point variables and constants must have values between $\pm 2^{17}$ (131072).

[true or false] The value 131070 is permissible in fixed-point calculations on the 7090. _____

true

1.158   You have been shown that a floating-point constant must be represented by the number itself with decimal point included (even when it is a whole-number quantity). A floating-point constant may also be represented in FORTRAN as an ordinary constant times a power of 10.

1.159   In ordinary notation, very large or small numbers are often noted this way: as in 3.5×10^7, which means 35000000. With FORTRAN constants this form may be used with the letter E following the constant, followed in turn by the desired power of 10, as in 3.5E + 7. (NOTE: the power of 10 must be expressed as a *fixed-point constant*.)

The FORTRAN constant 3.5E + 4 stands for a value (written out) of _____ .

35000.

1.160   The same notation may be used with negative powers of ten for very small numbers. For example, the constant 3.5E − 7 stands for the number

0.00000035. The general form is, again, any floating-point constant followed by the letter E followed, in turn, by the desired power of ten (positive or negative) by which the original constant is to be multiplied.

A shorthand version of the number 0.000001 might be _____. (Use the form described above with the smallest *whole*-number constant.)

1.E — 6

1.161 You might ask, "how is this form different from the double-asterisk sign, such as 10.** 6?" This very logical question is answered by the fact that the double-asterisk sign tells the computer to actually compute the indicated power while the E notation defines the number directly as in any constant.

Assuming that 10^{38} is the largest number permitted in the computer, show how a constant of this value would be represented in the E notation. _____

1.E38 (or 1.E + 38; the "plus" sign may be omitted)
   This example illustrates the usefulness of the E notation; without such a shorthand form, the number 10^{38} would be written

   100000000000000000000000000000000000000.

This completes the material on arithmetic formula statements. On the following pages you will find the examination for the chapter you have just finished.

PART 1: EXAMINATION

1. Given the following table of variable values:

Name	Value
A	1.0
B	3.0
C	5.0
D	2.0

Indicate each of the numeric values which the variable X would represent after the computer had completed each of the arithmetic formula statements below. (For example, the statement X = A + B + C + D would tell the computer to add 1.0, 3.0, 5.0, and 2.0 and set the value of X equal to 11.0.)

Statement		X value
(a)	X = C + D − 1.0	6.0
(b)	X = B * C * D	30.0
(c)	X = A + B/C	1.6
(d)	X = B + C − A − D	5.0
(e)	X = B * C/D * A	7.5
(f)	X = B * B/B	3.0
(g)	X = 3.0 * B ** 2 − B * C − A − D	9.0
(h)	X = X + A [assuming the computer has just executed (b) above]	31.0
(i)	X = D * D * D * D/32.0	0.5
(j)	X = −D	−2.0

2. Assume a projectile is launched from a reference point with coordinates (0, 0). It has an initial velocity v_x in the horizontal direction, and an initial vertical velocity of v_y. The x and y coordinate distances are governed by the following formulae:

$$x = (v_x)(t)$$
$$y = (v_y)(t) - 0.5(g)(t^2)$$

Where v_x and v_y are velocity in *feet per second,* t is the time in *seconds,* and g is the acceleration of gravity (32.174), and x and y come out in *feet.* Write a suitable pair of arithmetic formula statements to compute X and Y in *miles* (5280 feet per mile) assuming that suitable values exist for the variables VX, VY, G, and T.   X = VX * T/5280.
Y = (VY * T − 0.5 * G * T**2)/5280.

3. Consider the following sequence of arithmetic formula statements a "program" to be executed in the order in which they are written. After each statement has been executed show the current values of the variables A, B, and C, assuming each was originally zero.

38

	A	B	C
A = 5.0	5.0	0	0
B = −A	5.0	−5.0	0
C = A/B − 1.0	5.0	−5.0	−2.0
C = C + 1.0	5.0	−5.0	−1.0
B = B * B + C	5.0	24.0	−1.0
A = A ** 2 − B	1.0	24.0	−1.0
B = B − C + A	1.0	26.0	−1.0
C = B * C	1.0	26.0	−26.0
B = B/2.0	1.0	13.0	−26.0
A = C/B + 12.0	10.0	13.0	−26.0

4. Indicate which two variables and/or constants are involved in the *first* operation performed within the following expressions.

(a) A * X ** 2 + B * X + C: ___X___ ___2___
(b) X ** (A + B): ___A___ ___B___
(c) A ** (K ** (I + 1)): ___I___ ___1___
(d) A/B/C: ___A___ ___B___
(e) (((A + B) * X + C) * X + D) * X: ___A___ ___B___

5. Point out the "bug" in each of the following statements. (There is one, and only one, error in each.)

(a) X + Y = A: ___A = X + Y___
(b) V = I * R: ___I___
(c) N = N + 1.0: ___1___
(d) 3.1415926 = PI: ___PI = 3.1415926___
(e) J = N ** 1.5: ___1.5___ mixed mode.
(f) R = ((X ** 2) + Y ** 2)) ** 0.5: ___((X ** 2) + (Y ** 2)) ** 0.5___
(g) A = B ** N − 2: ___A = B ** (N − 2)___
(h) F = 1/(A + B + C): ___1.___
(i) TEMP = −RECORDS: ___S___
(j) A = K ** (J + 2N): _____

6. Given the formulas:

$$v_c = \frac{v_{cc}/R_L - i_L + b_1/R_1 + b_2/R_2 + b_3/R_3}{1/R_L + 1/R_1 + 1/R_2 + 1/R_3}$$

$$i_r = \frac{v_c - b_1}{R_1}$$

$$i_a = \frac{v_{cc} - v_c}{(R_L)(\beta)}$$

$$i_b = i_r - i_a$$

Write a suitable sequence of at least four arithmetic formula statements to compute these formulas, bearing in mind the fact that variables are being defined and used in subsequent formulas. Be careful not to assign a name of the wrong mode to a variable by misuse of the first letter. Assume that values already exist for all the variables except those four on the left of the equals sign. Do all arithmetic in the floating-point mode. NOTE: The subscripts shown above are merely part of the associated symbol, not positions in arrays.

7. Identify the incorrect subscript usage in one (and only one) of the following statements:

(a) A(I) = B(I) * C(I)
(b) J = N(K) ** (3 * K ** 2)
(c) B(L) = SAMPLE(4 * L − K)
(d) A(1) = B1 − ANUM(J)
(e) X = A(I) * B(J)/C(INDEX)   *Ans.* __(e)__

PART 2

CONTROL STATEMENTS

In the preceding chapter you were shown how to refer to quantities as constants, variables, or lists with FORTRAN notation, and how to involve these quantities in useful mathematical computation. Most programs require much more than this, however. Very few problems suitable for computer treatment can be solved by a simple sequence of formulas. In most cases the program must also involve decision making, error checking, and diagnostic procedures. Instead of writing the program in a "straight line," the programmer builds in "loops" and "branches." For these reasons FORTRAN provides a set of "control statements" to give the programmer the tools with which to provide these options. Part 2 will cover in detail the essential control statements provided by FORTRAN, and will mention in brief the remaining useful but nonessential ones.

2.1 The normal order of execution of statements by the computer is the order in which they are written. The statements

1   Y = A + 3. * B
2   X = X + Y

would tell the computer to execute statement 1 completely, then go on to execute statement 2.

In the example shown above, the variable named Y has its value defined in statement _____ .

1

2.2 This chapter will be devoted to the use of control statements with which the programmer can alter the normal order of execution of statements.

[true or false] Except where control statements are used, the order in which statements are executed by the computer is the order in which they are written.

_____

true

2.3 A control statement is, by definition, a statement which may cause the computer to execute a statement *other* than the next statement in sequence.

A control statement changes the _____ in which statements are executed.

order (or sequence)

2.4 You have observed that writing arithmetic formula statements permits considerable flexibility in assigning names and constructing expressions, etc., as long as you remain within the basic format. Most control statements, however, have rigid rules of wording, punctuation, and format which must be observed.

2.5   In order to tell the computer to execute an instruction which is not the next in the written sequence, there must be a way in which to refer to a specific statement in the program. This is accomplished by *statement numbers*.

FORTRAN statements may have _____ _____ in order that they may be referred to by other statements.

2.6   In FORTRAN programs any statement may be assigned a number. This number is arbitrarily chosen by the program writer and is placed to the left of the actual statement, as, for example:

$$100 \quad Y = A + 3. * B$$
$$1 \quad\quad X = X + Y$$

The second statement shown above has a statement number of _____.

2.7   The rules of statement numbering are simple; any statement may have an assigned number (no particular order of numbers is required) and, naturally, no two statements may have the same number.

Statement numbers are arbitrarily assigned numbers appearing on the _____ of the statement to which they refer.

2.8   Given the statements

$$1 \quad\quad X = 2.1059$$
$$3 \quad\quad A = 3.$$
$$3000 \quad B = 4.$$
$$2 \quad\quad Y = A * X ** 2 + B * X$$

the computer will proceed to execute them in the order written, 1, 3, 3000, and 2.

[true or false] The numerical value of a statement number has no bearing on the order of execution. _____

2.9   While any statement may have an arbitrarily assigned statement number, they are used in most cases only where a "label" is needed; that is, they are used where it is necessary to refer to that statement from some other part of the program.

[true or false] Arithmetic formula statements are the only statements which can have statement numbers. _____

2.10　Statement numbers are chosen in an arbitrary fashion, but they must not be larger in size than a certain upper limit. On the 7090, for example, statement numbers may not exceed the value of 32767.

33766 [is or is not] _____ a legal statement number in 7090 FORTRAN.

2.11　The principal use of statement numbers is to provide a *reference* for control statements. The control statement tells the computer which statement to execute next by referring to a statement number.

Statement numbers as labels are used chiefly by _____ statements.

2.12　The control statement enables the computer to make controlled "decisions." These decisions are always a choice of the next statement to be executed based on some elementary condition, such as whether a number is positive, negative, or zero. Part 2 will show how to use these decisions to control a program.

[true or false] The "decision" the computer makes is "which statement do I execute next?" _____

2.13　Since the computer can only decide where to go next in the program, it is up to the programmer to arrange the parts of the program in a logical order to take advantage of this control; that is, the statements must be grouped and ordered according to the effect you wish the decision to have.

One of the most useful decision-making statements is the IF statement. This statement *always* consists of the word IF followed by a pair of parentheses containing any desired expression, after which come *three* statement numbers. An example of an IF statement might be IF (X − Y)10,20,30.

The IF statement always contains exactly _____ statement numbers.

2.14　The IF statement tells the computer to do the following: "compute the entire expression contained in the parentheses; if the computed value is *negative* go next to the *first* indicated statement, if the value is *zero* go next to the *second* indicated statement or if the computed value is *positive* go next to the *third* statement."

In the example IF $(X - Y)$10,20,30, assume that the computed value of $(X - Y)$ is positive. When this IF statement is executed under those conditions, the next statement to be executed would be number _____ .

30

2.15 The computer's ability to select one of three possible successive statements as in the IF statement is often called "branching" or "conditional transfer." When the IF statement is executed the computer will "branch" on the condition of a negative, zero, or positive value for the indicated expression.

In the statement IF $(X ** 2 - 1.0)$30,20,10, if the value of X were -1.0 the computer would go next to statement number _____ when executing this statement.

20
(The expression $(X ** 2 - 1.)$ is *zero* for that value.)

2.16 The IF statement must conform exactly to the prescribed format, so let's look at that again. The statement consists of the word IF, followed by a pair of parentheses containing an expression (which may have additional parentheses), followed in turn by exactly three statement numbers.

[true or false] The statement IF $(X ** 3)$17,2,39,103 is a legal IF statement.

_____

false (too many options)

2.17 Notice that the statement numbers are separated by commas. Naturally there must be some way of clearly defining where one statement number ends and the next begins. However, there is no comma permitted either before the first statement number or after the last.

The statement IF $(X * Y - 25.)$5 6 7 can be made legitimate by the insertion of two _____ .

commas

2.18 It is possible to make a two-way branch with an IF statement by making two of the statement number options the same (three statement numbers in all are still required). For instance, the statement IF (A)7,7,8 will send the computer to statement 8 only if the value of A is positive and nonzero.

Regardless of the values of A, B, and C the computer, executing the statement IF (A + B − C)20,20,20, will always go next to statement number _____.

20
(Clearly this is nonsense; no useful decision would be made.)

2.19 The nonsense question of the preceding frame is intended to make a point; the IF statement will branch to either *three* alternative paths (if the indicated statement numbers are all different) or *two* alternative paths (if any two of the three numbers are alike), but it serves no purpose if all the numbers are alike.

If you wished to have the computer execute statement 100 if VALUE were a positive quantity or execute statement 200 if VALUE were other than positive, you would write the following statement: _____.

IF (VALUE)200,200,100

2.20 An IF statement, like any FORTRAN statement, may have a statement number of its own for reference by other statements. An IF statement is not allowed to branch to itself, however; such a condition could obviously be disastrous. Think what would happen in the statement 3   IF (A)1,2,3 if A were positive!

If the variable A in the statement sample shown above were positive, the computer would go on executing statement _____ until the computer fell apart (or somebody pulled the plug).

3

2.21 In an IF statement, the expression whose value is to be tested may be as simple or complex as desired. It may contain parentheses of its own but it must be completely contained in a pair of parentheses belonging to the IF statement itself.

[true or false] The statement IF ((A + B) * C)2,2,3 is a legal IF statement. _____

true

2.22 Write a statement to test the expression A(J) ** 3 − TEST. If the computed value is negative, the computer should execute statement 39 next; otherwise the computer should go to statement 1. _____

IF (A(J) ** 3 − TEST)39,1,1
If your answer agrees with the one shown above, go to page 47 and read frame 2.25. If you did not get the correct answer, continue with frame 2.23.

2.23   This problem was obviously intended for an IF statement. Write down the word IF and an open parenthesis; follow this with the tested expression and the balancing closing parenthesis. Next comes the group of statement numbers which indicate the branch directions.

2.24   If the expression's value was negative in this problem the computer was to go next to statement 39; otherwise, statement 1 was to be executed next. The order of statement number options always corresponds to *negative, zero,* or *positive* expression values, respectively. Thus 39,1,1 is the proper sequence of statement numbers for this problem. The complete statement to fulfill the requirements of this sample problem is:

$$\text{IF } (A(J) ** 3 - \text{TEST})39,1,1$$

Write a statement that the computer will execute statement 27 next if $A * X ** 2 - C ** (J - 1)$ has a value of *zero* and statement 28 if other than zero. _____

IF $(A * X ** 2 - C ** (J - 1))28,27,28$
   If your answer agrees with the one shown above (including at least this many parentheses) go on to frame 2.25. If your answer is incorrect, better review all the material up to this point on IF statements, starting with frame 2.13.

2.25   One very common application of the IF statement is to determine if a computed quantity is less than, equal to, or greater than another quantity. This is done by writing the expression as a difference of the two quantities so that the resulting value will be negative, zero, or positive.

In the statement IF $(X - 3.0)20,30,40$, the computer is told to go next to statement _____ if the value of X is greater than 3.0.

40
   Since $(X - 3.0) > 0.$

2.26   The example of the preceding frame showed a variable compared with a constant. The same method can be applied to two variables (or more) as in the example IF $(X - Y)1,2,5$.

The computer, when executing the above statement, will go next to statement 1 if the value of X is _____ than the value of Y.

less
   (Since the result is negative.)

2.27   In review, the IF statement instructs the computer to compute an expression, just as it would to begin an arithmetic formula statement execution, and select the part of the program to which it will go next depending on whether the value of the computation is negative, zero, or positive.

EXERCISE 2.1

Given four variables, A, B, C, and D, with previously defined values, write a sequence of IF statements to tell the computer to execute statement 15 if *all four* variables have the exact value of 25.0. If one or more variables has a different value, tell the computer to execute statement 30 instead.

IF (A − 25.0) 30,15, 30   IF (B − 25.0) 30,15,30   IF (C − 25.0) 30,15,30
                                                  IF (D − 25.0) 30,15,30

2.28   One important point: the value of the computed expression is lost as soon as the computer has completed the IF statement. The expression in the IF statement is simply a series of operations resulting in a single computed value and does not imply that a variable will contain this value as in the arithmetic formula statement.

[true or false] At the conclusion of the execution of the IF statement the value of the computed expression is then available for future statements. _____

> false

2.29   To illustrate this point consider the statement IF (A * B − C)1,1,2 which will instruct the computer to compute the expression A * B − C and pick out its next statement according to the usual rule. The value of A * B − C is no longer available to future statements unless it is recomputed by an arithmetic formula statement, resulting in duplication of effort and wasted time.

[true or false] After executing the statement IF (X − Y)10,20,30, the computed value of X − Y is not available and must be recomputed if needed in future statements. _____

> true

2.30   The programmer should give a lot of thought before writing a complicated expression in an IF statement. He should first determine if he needs that computed value in other statements; if so, the expression should be computed in an arithmetic formula statement prior to executing the IF in order to avoid wasted motion.

Given the statement IF (Z − G)10,25,1001, and the value of −1.0 for Z and −2.0 for G, what statement would the computer execute after the statement shown above? _____

> 1001 (Z − G > 0)

2.31   The statements SAMPLE = X ** 2 − B * Z and IF (SAMPLE)10,20,30, executed in that order, will have the same effect as IF (X ** 2 − B * Z)10,20,30; in the first case, however, the value of the expression is saved in the variable SAMPLE and will be available for future statements' use.

If the variables X, B, and Z in the example above each had a value of 2.0, the computer would select its next executed statement (in either case) as statement number _____ .

2.32   Remember that the parentheses of an IF statement contain an *expression* subject to all the rules of hierarchy and mode that apply to expressions in arithmetic formula statements. In particular, remember that the expressions may only contain quantities of the same mode, except for exponents and subscripts.

[true or false] The statement IF (HENRY + HOMER — JIM)1,2,3 is a legal IF statement. _____

The IF statement, then, contains three elements:

The word IF.
An expression contained in parentheses.
Three statement numbers indicating alternate paths for the computer.

All IF statements are constructed in this basic form, with just the few simple rules stated above to follow.

EXERCISE 2.2

Assume that values have been computed for three variables X, Y, and Z. (No two values alike.) If the value of X is:

handwritten: IF $(X - Y)2, , 1$

(a)   Greater than *both* Y *and* Z go to statement 10   *handwritten:* IF $(X - Z)30, , 10$
(b)   Less than Y but greater than Z go to statement 20
(c)   Greater than Y but less than Z go to statement 30 *handwritten:* IF $(X - Z)40, , 20$
(d)   Less than *both* Y *and* Z go to statement 40

Write a sequence of IF statements to make the decisions outlined above. (The second statement number option is irrelevant in each IF statement since it is given that no two values are alike.)

2.33   Now that you know everything about IF statements, let's look at a few examples to show how they are used in FORTRAN programs. For example, suppose you wish to compute the square root of the quantity called X, and you must first make sure that X is a positive quantity. The use of the IF statement to accomplish this is illustrated in the next frame.

2.34   Sample program segment:

$$IF\ (X)40,30,30$$
$$40\quad X = -X$$
$$30\quad ROOT = X ** 0.5$$

If the value of X were a negative number, statement _____ would be executed to change its sign.

2.35   When statement 40 of the preceding example is executed by the computer, the value of X will have its sign changed and the computer will continue on to statement 30   ROOT = X ** 0.5 to compute the root. If the value of X had originally been positive, statement 30 would have been executed immediately.

The decision made by the IF statement of the preceding example was to ensure that the quantity whose square root was being computed was a _____ (sign) number.

2.36   The example above also illustrates two statements worthy of mention. The statement X = −X is a perfectly legal arithmetic formula statement; the original value of X has its sign changed and the new quantity replaces that value in X. The statement ROOT = X ** 0.5 shows the use of the exponent 0.5 to compute the square root.

2.37   One common characteristic of good computer programming is the ability to reexecute a statement or sequence of statements in a process called a "loop." A basic series of operations may be defined by a sequence of statements which the computer will execute a number of times with different values of the variables involved.

A basic sequence of operations which are executed repeatedly is called a _____.

2.38   The IF statement can be a valuable aid in controlling the progress of a loop. The example in the following frame will illustrate the use of the IF statement to compute "X factorial" which is defined as the product of the quantities X, X − 1, X − 2, X − 3, and so on down to 1. For example, 4 factorial is (4)(3)(2)(1) = 24. We assume that the floating-point quantity X has a whole-number value.

2.39   Sample program segment:

$$FACT = 1.0$$
$$Y = X$$
$$10 \quad FACT = FACT * Y$$
$$Y = Y - 1.0$$
$$IF \ (Y)20,20,10$$
$$20 \quad (Continue \ on \ in \ the \ program)$$

2.40   Have you studied the program in 2.39 thoroughly? Here is the explanation. The first two statements are initialization steps; FACT = 1.0 prepares the variable FACT for the first multiplication and Y = X gives us a working variable Y such that the value of X is preserved.

[true or false] The two statements described above are executed just once in the program segment shown in the preceding frame. _____

2.41   The statements

$$10 \quad FACT = FACT * Y$$
$$Y = Y - 1.0$$
$$IF \ (Y)20,20,10$$

represent the actual loop; the first time through, FACT becomes (1.) * (Y) and Y is reduced by 1.

If Y had an initial value of 10.0 the IF statement would transfer to statement _____ the first time through this loop.

2.42   Sample program segment:

$$FACT = 1.0$$
$$Y = X$$
$$10 \quad FACT = FACT * Y$$
$$Y = Y - 1.0$$
$$IF \ (Y)20,20,10$$
$$20 \quad (Continue \ on \ in \ the \ program)$$

2.43   The loop described in the preceding frame will continue repeating, accumulating the successive products in the variable FACT as the factorial definition prescribes, reducing the working variable Y by steps of 1.0, and testing so that when Y has a value of zero the loop is finished and the computer will go to statement 20.

Looking at the sample program segment discussed above, if the variable X had a value of 10.0, how many times would statement 10 be executed? _____

2.44   If you answered that last question correctly, you are grasping this loop concept pretty well. The idea of a loop in a program is to avoid writing similar statements over and over, wasting your time and energy and the computer's space and energy as well. One basic set of statements with proper control will often do the job.

Statement 20 in the foregoing example will be executed a total of _____ time(s).

2.45   Another use of the IF statement might be testing a counter where a loop is to be cycled a prescribed number of times. The next few frames will describe such a program which will compute the sum of an arithmetic progression. If you are familiar with the term "arithmetic progression" you may skip to frame 2.47.

2.46   An arithmetic progression is simply an ordered sequence of numbers which differ by the same amount. The series 1,2,3,4,5,6,7,8,9,10, . . . , is an arithmetic progression, as is 1,3,5,7,9, ... An arithmetic progression beginning with 2 having a difference of 4 would be 2,6,10,14,18, ... A progression usually has a definite number of terms also. The arithmetic progression beginning with 1 having ten terms and a difference of 2 would be: 1,3,5,7,9,11,13,15,17,19.

2.47   A program, or sequence of statements, to compute the sum of all the terms of any arithmetic progression must be given the following information: the first number, the difference, and the number of terms involved. Assume that the variables FIRST, DIF, and NUM respectively represent these quantities in the following example, and that they have been given values from some other part of the program.

2.48   Sample program segment:

```
        SUM = FIRST
        I = 1
10   FIRST = FIRST + DIF
        SUM = SUM + FIRST
        I = I + 1
        IF (I − NUM)10,20,20
20   (Continue on in the program)
```

52

2.49   Have you studied the sample program segment above? Here is the explanation. The first two statements are initialization, setting SUM equal to the first term in the progression and setting the counter to one. The loop itself begins with statement 10.

The first two statements of the sample program segment are executed _____ time(s) each.

one

2.50   The next four statements 10 FIRST = FIRST + DIF, SUM = SUM + FIRST, I = I + 1, and IF (I − NUM)10,20,20, constitute the loop such that the variable SUM has the quantity FIRST added to it each time through the loop and the counter I is increased by 1 each time through. As soon as the variable I has attained a value equal to NUM the loop is terminated by passing on to statement 20.

If NUM has a value of 15 in the loop shown above, statement 10 will be executed a total of _____ times. (Careful, now!)

14

2.51   Statement 10 in the sample program is executed one less time than the value of NUM since I has a value of 2 by the time the IF statement is executed the *first* time and will consequently have a value equal to NUM after "NUM−1" cycles through the loop and will go on to statement 20 at that time.

When statement 20 of this example is executed, the variable I will have a value of _____ . (assuming NUM has a value of 15)

15

2.52   This was admittedly a trivial example (the problem is better solved by direct substitution in a formula) but it was intended chiefly to illustrate the loop concept. IF statements can control the progress of a loop either by testing a counter or some other computed quantity in the loop to determine when to exit the loop.

$$I = 0$$
$$10 \ INDEX \ (I) = I$$
$$I = I + 1$$
$$IF \ (I - 2000) \ 10, 20, 20$$
$$20. \ Continue$$

EXERCISE 2.3

Write a program to set each value of an array called INDEX equal to the order of that value in the array (that is, INDEX (1) = 1, INDEX (2) = 2, etc.). The INDEX array has a total length of 2000 numbers.

2.53   The IF statement is one of the simplest and yet most powerful of the control statements. Another very simple statement which is discussed in the next few frames is the GO TO statement.

2.54   The GO TO statement consists of the two words GO TO followed by a single statement number. When a GO TO statement is executed the computer is told to execute next the indicated statement. For example, the statement GO TO 12 will tell the computer to go next to statement 12.

After executing the statement GO TO 1000 the computer will execute statement number _____ next.

1000

2.55   The use of the GO TO statement is often called "unconditional branching" or "unconditional transfer" since no choice is made by the computer. Actually the GO TO statement usually appears at the end of a sequence of statements representing an option of some other control statement, and serves to direct the computer back to some other part of the program, or to skip some portion of the program.

2.56   Sample program segment:

```
            IF (X − Y) 10,20,30
     10   · · · (Some statement or sequence of statements)
          GO TO 40
     20   · · · (Some statement or sequence of statements)
          GO TO 40
     30   · · · (Some statement or sequence of statements)
     40   (Continue on in the program)
```

2.57   The sample program segment above shows an IF statement directing the computer to one of three options. No matter which path the computer takes, the GO TO statements will eventually direct the computer to statement 40. Notice that, in this case, the third path does not need a GO TO statement since the program naturally arrives at statement 40 without requiring control.

In the GO TO statement, the words GO TO are always followed by a _____ _____ .

statement number

2.58   You have been shown some of the uses of two of the members of the control statement family. Both of these statements have the ability to tell the computer to go somewhere other than to the next statement as it normally would. The IF statement provides *conditional* branching while the GO TO statement involves *unconditional* branching. You are about to meet the king of all the control statements: the DO statement.

2.59 As previously discussed, we can make a program with a loop in which an IF statement is used to test the value of a counter. The counter, in that case, is a variable which is increased in value each time a pass through the loop is made.

The loop approach described above requires stepping and testing a variable called a _____ .

2.60 To construct a loop using a counter and an IF statement to test its status requires separate statements to step the counter and test its current value. FORTRAN provides a powerful statement to keep track of both operations in controlling a loop: the DO statement.

2.61 The DO statement is constructed in the following form: the word DO followed by a statement number which is followed, in turn, by an index definition. An example of a DO statement might be DO 10 I = 1, 100 where 10 is the statement number and I = 1, 100 is the index definition.

The DO statement always begins with the word _____ .

2.62 The index definition (e.g. I = 1, 100) is always made up of a non-subscripted, *fixed-point* variable followed by an equals sign and at least two *fixed-point* quantities separated by a comma.

[true or false] The index definition ANUM = 1,1000 is valid according to the above definition. _____

2.63 The DO statement tells the computer to "repeatedly execute the *successive* sequence of statements up to and including the statement whose number appears in the DO, cycling the index each time through according to the index definition." That is, all those statements following the DO represent a loop.

The statement DO 10 I = 1, 100 will cause the computer to repeatedly execute the statements following the DO up to and including statement _____ .

2.64 The index definition (e.g. I = 1, 100) indicates that the variable on the left of the equals sign is set equal to the first quantity on the right of the equals sign for the first pass through the loop, and the variable's value is increased by 1

55

on each successive pass until it reaches a value equal to the second quantity on the right of the equals sign.

The index definition shown above would cause the variable I to take on values from _____ to _____ .

2.65 The DO statement, then, controls a loop by causing the computer to repeatedly execute the statements *following* the DO up to and including the indicated statement, beginning with the index variable set equal to the first indicated value and increasing its value until it equals the second indicated value, at which time the loop ends and the computer continues on in the program.

The statement DO 20 K = 1,50 will execute the statements through 20 a total of _____ times.

2.66 Consider an example. The statement DO 10 I = 1, 100 tells the computer to start with the very next statement and execute all the statements down to and including statement 10, having given the variable I a value of 1. When statement 10 has been reached the computer will go back to the first statement *after* the DO and repeat, having increased the value of I by 1. This goes on until I reaches 100.

On the pass in which I of the above example reaches 100, the computer will go on to the statement immediately after statement _____ when it finishes the loop.

2.67 The format of the DO statement is very important, so let's review that again: the word DO, a statement number (warning: no comma allowed at this point, normal as that may appear), a fixed-point variable, an equals sign, and, lastly, at least two fixed-point quantities separated by a comma.

Identify the valid DO statements below by a plus sign; indicate the incorrect ones with a minus sign.

DO 111 III = 1,1111 _____   DO 100 A = 10,20   _____
DO 10, J = 1,10   _____   DO A12I = NO, NONO   _____

2.68 The quantities to the right of the equals sign in the index definition may be fixed-point constants or fixed-point variables whose values are computed elsewhere. Thus, DO 5 I = 1, K, DO 215 JOB = N, 100, and DO 100 L = L1, L2, are all examples of legal DO statements.

Assume K equals 10 in the first example above. The computer will loop through statement 5 a total of _____ times.

2.69 The use of variables on the right of the equals sign in an index definition permits the programmer to construct a loop whose number of cycles can be changed by a computation in the program (outside the loop). If you attempt to alter these values during the loop execution, it will have no effect, as the limits are already set.

DO 5 I = 1,2 will cause the computer to loop through statement 5 a total of _____ times.

2.70 Once again, be warned that the DO statement format must be strictly observed. No comma is permitted between the statement number and the index definition. Also, fixed-point constants or variables are permitted as index defining limits, but no expression involving a mathematical operation is permitted.

[true or false] The statement DO 10 I = 1, N − 1 is a legal DO statement.

2.71 The first quantity on the right of the equals sign in the index definition (lower index limit) must be a smaller value than the second number (upper index limit) since the index will always be counted *upward*. If this rule is not observed, the loop will still cycle *once* (with the lower limit value) and then drop out.

The loop described by DO 15 N = 10,1 will be executed one time with a value of _____ for N.

2.72 The index definition permits a third quantity on the right of the equals sign. If it is desired that the index count up in steps other than one unit at a time, the desired step value may be written in the DO statement as the third quantity in the index definition, separated from the upper limit value by a comma.

The *first* time through the loop prescribed by DO 5 I = 5,10 the variable I will have a value of _____ .

2.73 If, for example, you wished the index variable in a DO loop to take on the values of 1, 3, 5, 7, ... , 99, you might write a DO statement as DO 8 I = 1,99,2 which would cause the index variable I to start with a value of 1 and loop repeatedly, adding 2 to its value each time through the loop.

When the index variable in the example above reaches a value of _____ the loop will be completed.

2.74 If the third quantity in the index definition is specified to be other than 1, it would be possible to have a situation in which the index variable would never reach the exact value of the upper limit. (For example, I = 1,100,2.) In this case, the loop is terminated when the index reaches the largest possible value without exceeding the upper limit. (In this example, 99.)

In the statement DO 10 I = 1,11,3 the largest value attained by the index I would be _____ .

2.75 This third quantity in the index definition is called the *index increment* and the complete format of the index definition can be stated: an *index variable,* an *equals sign,* a *lower limit,* an *upper limit,* and an optional *increment.* These last three items may be either constants or variables, but not expressions involving operations. If the increment is not otherwise specified, it is taken to be one as in the original definition.

2.76 The actual procedure used by the computer in interpreting a DO statement is as follows: set the index variable equal to the indicated first value (lower limit) and execute all the statements up to and including the indicated statement; increase the index variables value by the indicated increment (or one if none specified) and check the current value against the upper limit; if the index is less than or equal to the indicated upper limit, go back and reexecute the loop; if the index has reached a value greater than the upper limit, drop out of the loop.

2.77 Actually the DO *statement* is thought of as being executed *once* while its prescribed loop sequence is being cycled according to the DO control. Incidentally, a loop under control of a DO statement is usually referred to as a "DO-loop."

The loop prescribed by the statement DO 1 I = 10,10 will be executed once with a value of _____ for the index.

2.78   The next few frames will describe a simple example of the use of the DO-loop. The problem is to find the sum of all the numbers in a list of numbers called A which contains a total of 50 numbers.

2.79   Sample program segment:

$$\text{SUM} = 0.0$$
$$\text{DO } 10 \text{ I} = 1,50$$
$$10 \quad \text{SUM} = \text{SUM} + \text{A(I)}$$

2.80   Have you studied the sample program segment above? Here is the explanation. The variable SUM is initialized to a value of 0.0 (this variable will be used to accumulate the sum of the list called A); the DO statement then controls a loop of one statement, reexecuting that statement 50 times. Each time statement 10 is executed the value of I, the index variable, is increased by 1 such that the reference to A(I) will refer each time to a successive number in the A list. When the loop is completed, SUM will contain the desired sum of the A's.

2.81   This example program illustrates a number of notable points. First of all, the use of the index variable is definitely permitted within the loop itself. In fact this is a very desirable feature of the DO-loop and many instances will arise where the index value is useful as a subscript, exponent, etc.

In the preceding example, the statements DO 10 I = 1,50 and 10   SUM = SUM + A(I) show the use of the index variable I as both a counter and a _____ .

2.82   The only restriction on the use of the index variable within the loop is that you do *not* change its value in any way such as using it on the left of an arithmetic formula statement. It may be used as a term or factor in an expression if desired, but remember that it is a fixed-point quantity and you may have to change its mode.

The fixed-point value of I may be converted to floating-point in the variable XI by the arithmetic formula statement _____ .

2.83   The second item of note in the sample program is the use of a variable as an accumulator for a summing process. The statement SUM = SUM + A(I) has been used in this way such that each time this statement is executed under the DO control a new number of the A array is added into the current sum. At the conclusion of the loop, SUM contains the desired result. This is a commonly used technique.

[true or false] In order to use the above mentioned summing technique, the variable SUM *must* first be initialized to zero. _____

true

2.84 Any FORTRAN statements may be used in a DO-loop but the loop must *not* end with a control statement of any kind. If it is necessary to conclude a DO-loop with a controlled decision, a dummy statement must be used after the control statement, as in the following example.

$$DO\ 10\ I = 1,15$$
$$IF\ (A(I) - 1.)\ 10,20,10$$
$$10\quad CONTINUE$$

2.85 The dummy statement used at the end of a DO-loop is the CONTINUE statement, consisting simply of the word CONTINUE. Its use will be demonstrated in the following program which will determine the largest number in an array of numbers called A which contains 1000 numbers.

2.86 Sample program segment:

$$BIGA = A(1)$$
$$10\quad DO\ 50\ I = 2,1000$$
$$20\quad IF\ (A(I) - BIGA)\ 50,50,30$$
$$30\quad BIGA = A(I)$$
$$50\quad CONTINUE$$

2.87 Have you studied the above program? Here is the explanation. BIGA, the variable whose value will eventually be the largest number in A, is first set equal to A(1) to be used as a basis for comparison. The DO-loop then compares the current BIGA value with successive numbers in the A array. The IF statement that does this either goes to statement 30 if the new A value is larger (and then replaces the old BIGA value), or goes to statement 50 if the A value is not larger than the current BIGA. When the loop is finished, BIGA is the desired value.

2.88 The reason for the existence of the CONTINUE statement is to provide the common finishing point for the DO-loop. Remember, the definition of the DO statement required that the computer execute the statements *through* the one indicated in the DO statement. This type of problem which involves branching in the loop often requires the use of a CONTINUE statement to provide this finishing point.

A DO-loop cannot end with a _____ (type) statement.

2.89   Look again at the sample program. Notice that the IF statement needs someplace to go if the new A value is not larger than the current BIGA value. The IF statement cannot go back to the DO statement without starting the loop over again; therefore, it must have someplace to go forward in the program, namely the last statement in the loop as prescribed by the DO definition.

2.90   The CONTINUE statement actually does nothing in the execution of the program; that is, it doesn't tell the computer to do anything. It merely serves the purpose of providing the DO statement with a reference number in a loop which might otherwise end with a control statement.

2.91   [true or false] Regardless of how many branch directions there are in a DO loop, all the possible paths must lead to a single particular statement at the end of the loop. _____

2.92   All in all, the DO statement is a pretty simple one once you become familiar with the little details. All of the statements which comprise the loop must be between the DO statement and the statement whose number appears in the DO. You may tell the computer to jump around inside the loop, but all paths must eventually lead to the statement marking the end of the loop.

EXERCISE 2.4

Write a DO-loop to find the smallest absolute value in a block of 100 numbers called X. Use a variable called SMALLX for this quantity. Assume the first number in the block is positive if you wish.

2.93   A branching statement may cause the computer to leave a DO-loop before the index has completely cycled in the normal fashion. When this happens the index value is available for use in subsequent statements, and usually when such a situation occurs this value is of interest, as in the following example to locate the first occurrence of the number zero in an array called BLOCK which contains 2000 numbers.

$SMALL X = X(1)$
$DO\ 40\ I = \{2, 100\}$
$IF\ (X(1))\ 10, 20, 20$
$10\qquad X(I) = -X(I)$
$20\quad IF\ (X(I) - SMALL X)\ 30, 40, 40$
$30\qquad SMALL X = X(I)$
$40\qquad CONTINUE$

2.94   Sample program segments:

```
      ┌    DO 10 I = 1,2000
      │    IF (BLOCK(I))10,20,10
      └ 10 CONTINUE
        11 LOC = 0
           GO TO 21
        20 LOC = I
        21 (Continue on in program)
```

NOTE: brackets will be used in future sample program segments to outline DO-loops, as done in this frame, for clarification purposes.

2.95   The DO-loop in the above example simply tests successive numbers in the BLOCK array, the IF statement going to statement 10 to repeat the loop until a zero is found in BLOCK. At this time the IF statement goes to statement 20 where I (the location in BLOCK where zero was found) has its value saved in LOC. If the loop goes all the way through BLOCK and does not find a zero, the computer goes to the statement after 10, which sets LOC to zero (to indicate that BLOCK does not have the desired number) and hops on in the program.

2.96   The sample program of frame 2.94 serves to demonstrate a jump out of a loop before the index cycle is complete. This will be called a "special exit" while the ordinary condition of leaving a DO-loop by completing the index cycle will be called a "normal exit" (as when statement 11 is reached).

If a value of zero is found in BLOCK in this example, the computer will do a _____ exit from the loop.

special

2.97   As demonstrated in the example of frame 2.94, when a special exit is made the current value of the DO index is intact and may be used in any desired way. If a normal exit is made, however, there is no guarantee that the index value is meaningful. This is no special problem, since in a normal exit the index upper limit is known.

[true or false] In the sample program of frame 2.94, if no zero value is found in BLOCK, statement 20 will not be executed. _____

true

2.98   The statements following the DO statement up to the statement indicated in the DO itself are called the "range" of the DO-loop. There are certain strict rules about the ranges of DO-loops which are mentioned in the next few frames.

The range of the statement DO 1010 INDEX = I,J,K extends through statement _____ .

2.99   The first rule concerning DO-loop ranges states that you are not allowed to transfer (e.g. IF or GO TO) to any statement *inside* the range of a DO from *outside* its range. You can transfer to a DO statement itself, but not to any statement in its range; those statements are under control of the DO only.

[true or false] The sequence DO 10 I = 1, 100; 10 A(I) = B(I); GO TO 10 is legal. _____

2.100   A second rule about ranges states that a DO-loop may exist completely inside the range of another DO-loop. When this structure is used, the innermost loop must be entirely contained by the outer loop; in other words, the loops must not overlap in any way. (This condition of loops within loops is further explained a little later.)

[true or false] The sequence DO 10 I = 1, 1000···DO 20 J = 1, 10···10 CONTINUE···20 CONTINUE is illegal because the second DO-loop extends beyond the range of the first. _____

2.101   The arrow diagram below shows some of the legal branch conditions in DO-loops (numbers 1, 2, and 3) and also shows some of the illegal cases (numbers 4 and 5). The arrows simply show direction of transfer.

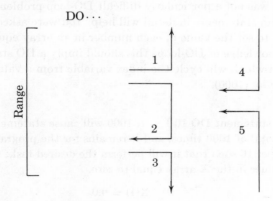

63

2.102   The arrow diagram below shows some legal (1, 2, 3, and 4) and illegal (5 to 10) branch conditions in nested DO-loops:

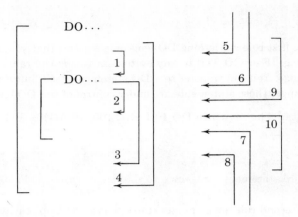

Write a one-statement DO-loop to set all the number values in a 1000-number array called X equal to zero.

10 _____

Use I for the index variable name and statement 10 for the range of the loop.

> DO 10 I = 1, 1000
> 10   X(I) = 0.0
>
> If your answer agrees with the one shown, skip to Exercise 2.5. If your answer does not agree with this one, continue with frame 2.103.

2.103   This was not a particularly difficult DO-loop problem. Perhaps going over the problem statements in detail will help. You were asked to write a one-statement loop to set the value of each number in an array equal to zero. With your present knowledge of DO-loops this should imply a DO statement with an index definition which will cycle the index variable from a value of 1 up to the length of the array (1000).

2.104   The statement DO 10 I = 1, 1000 will cause statement number 10 to be executed a total of 1000 times, and it remains for the programmer to specify statement number 10 such that it will perform the desired task: setting the value of successive values in the X array equal to zero.

10   X(I) = 0.0

(NOTE: the zero could be written a number of ways, as long as the decimal point is included to make it a floating-point constant.)

2.105   Each time the statement 10   X(I) = 0.0 is executed under control of the DO, the index I has a value larger by 1 than the previous time. Thus X(I) refers to successive numbers in the X array each time the statement is executed, as follows: X(1), X(2), X(3), X(4), . . . , X(1000).

2.106   The basic use of DO statements should be clear by now, and if you feel that you understand the makeup of this statement you may turn to the next frame and continue. If any points need clarifying, you had better review this material starting at frame 2.61.

$$DO \ 10 \ I = 1, 1000$$
$$10 \qquad A(I) = B(1001 - I)$$

EXERCISE 2.5

Write a DO-loop to copy the contents of an array called A into an array called B, both of which are 1000 numbers long, placing the numbers in the reverse order of that which they occupied in the original array. That is, B(1000) will contain A(1), B(999) will contain A(2), etc.

2.107   A few frames back it was mentioned that DO-loops containing other DO-loops is a situation commonly called "nesting" of loops. Under these circumstances the outer loop is begun first and, during its first pass, it gives control to the inner loop, which completely cycles itself before restoring control to the outer loop.

[true or false] When control passes to an inside loop it remains there until the loop is completely cycled. ____T____

true

2.108   When an outside loop regains control from an inner loop it continues through its pass, reaching the end and repeating as usual. In the course of its next pass it again will completely cycle the inner loop. This same thing happens on all subsequent passes. If this seems complicated, take heart; a simple analogy will be given in the next frame to give a better picture.

[true or false] With nested loops, the inner loop is completely cycled each time a pass is made through the outer loop. ____T____

true

2.109   Picture the following situation. Suppose you were walking around the grounds of an amusement park in a circular fashion. Each time you pass the merry-go-round you get on and take a complete ride (a certain number of times around the circle). That ride would be analogous to an inner loop and the walk to an outer loop.

[true or false] In this analogy the inner loop is completely cycled each time through the outer loop. ___T___

2.110 To carry this parallel one step further: if you decided to jump off the merry-go-round before it stopped, you might continue walking around the park or you might decide to jump out completely and go home. These cases correspond to permitted branch situations in nested DO-loops.

If you got off the ride before it stopped this would be equivalent to a ___special___ exit while if you were to wait for the merry-go-round to finish its run this would be the same as a ___normal___ exit in DO-loops.

2.111 There is practically no limit to the degree of nesting of DO-loops, although problems seldom arise that require more than two or three loops within loops. Quite often you will want to use DO-loops end-to-end inside another DO-loop (sort of like a merry-go-round and a ferris wheel in our carnival analogy).

The sequence DO 10 I = 1,10, DO 10 J = 1,10, 10   A(I) = A(I) + B(J) will cause statement 10 to be executed a total of ___100___ times.

2.112 When a special exit is made from an inner loop of a nested set of loops, the index values of all the external loops are preserved and available for use, including, of course, the index of the exited loop. An example of nested DO-loops follows, demonstrating this principle. This program looks through two arrays seeking the first duplication of values between the arrays and this location (index) is recorded in the arrays.

2.113 Sample program segment:

```
        DO 10 I = 1,10
        DO 10 J = 1,10
        IF (A(I) − B(J))10,20,10
    10  CONTINUE
        GO TO 30
    20  LOC(1) = I
        LOC(2) = J
    30  (Continue on in program)
```

2.114 Have you studied the above program? Here is the explanation. The outer DO sets I equal to 1 and goes to the second DO statement, setting J equal to 1. Thus the IF statement compares A(1) and B(1) the first time through. The inner DO then sets J equal to 2 (I is still 1) and compares again, and so on until J equals 10. At this time the value of I is increased to 2 and the inner loop begins again, J going from 1 to 10. When the first occurrence of equal A and B values is encountered, the IF statement will jump out to 20 and record the locations (index values).

2.115 You will notice that, even when two nested DO-loops end at the same statement as in this example, control is passed to the outer loop only when the inner loop has completed its index cycle. Thus it is perfectly permissible for the two loops to end their respective ranges on the same CONTINUE, as done here.

If the IF statement in the example of frame 2.113 causes a special exit to statement 20 during the 14th time it is executed, the values placed in LOC(1) and LOC(2) are, respectively, ___2___ and ___4___ .

2,4

2.116 If you were able to correctly answer the previous question, you are showing excellent progress and you may continue to the next frame immediately. Here is the explanation. If the IF statement is executed 14 times in that program, we know that the inner loop was completely cycled once (10 executions of the IF) and has gone 4 times through on the *second* execution of the outer loop; hence, I has a value of 2 and J a value of 4.

EXERCISE 2.6

Write a DO-loop to make a count of all the numbers greater than 10.0 in a 1000-number array called A. Use N as the name of the count variable and I as the loop index.

```
        N = 0
     DO 30 I = 1,1000
     IF (A(I) - 10.0) 30,30,20
 20  N = N + 1
 30  CONTINUE
```

2.117 One important note: the index variables in *nested* DO-loops must be different in name; that is, you are not allowed to use the same index for two DO-loops if one contains the other. However, there is no reason why you cannot use the same variable name in sequential DO-loops, since the index variable is free for any desired use in the program once a DO-loop is through with it.

[true or false] The sequence DO 5 I = 1, 200,   DO 5 X = 1,40,2,   5 (some statement) is legal. ___F___

---

false
    The index variables, though different, must both be fixed-point.

2.118 One last example of nested DO-loops will demonstrate the use of the outer loop's index variable to determine the inner loop's index limits. In this program, the outer loop is actually a counter to reexecute the inner loop a sufficient number of times to complete its function, which is to sort an array of numbers into numerical order.

2.119   Sample program segment:

```
        DO 100 I = 1, N
        K = N - I
        DO 100 J = 1, K
        IF (ARRAY(J) - ARRAY(J + 1))100,100,10
    10  TEMP = ARRAY(J)
        ARRAY(J) = ARRAY(J + 1)
        ARRAY(J + 1) = TEMP
   100  CONTINUE
```

2.120   The program shown above uses the technique of comparing adjacent numbers in an array, reversing the numbers if they are not in the correct numerical sequence. The first time through the loop ARRAY(1) is compared to ARRAY(2), the second time ARRAY(2) is compared to ARRAY(3), etc. Thus if the largest value of the array were in the first position, by the time the program had finished the inner loop once it would be in the last position in the list (with each number moved down one slot). This will happen, in fact, no matter where the largest number is.

2.121   After the inner loop is completely cycled once, the outer loop's index I changes its value to 2 and the inner loop begins again with a new upper index limit. This means that the inner loop is cycled one less time, resulting in one less comparison of number pairs. This is possible because the largest number in the array is already in correct position at the top of the list and need not be checked again.

2.122   Each complete execution of the inner loop will result in the largest of the remaining numbers in the array ending up at the highest available position in the list, no matter where it was located before the sorting began. Thus the completion of this sample program finds the list called ARRAY sorted into numerical order.

In the sample program of frame 2.119, if N (the length of the array to be sorted) has a value of 100, the inner loop will have an upper index limit of _____ ~~100~~ 99 the first time it is executed.

99

2.123   The IF statement in the inner loop of the sample program shown checks the successive pairs of numbers in ARRAY and, if they are in correct order (or equal) they are not changed and the loop begins again; however, if they are in reverse order, statement 10 is called on to reverse the position of these numbers in ARRAY.

If ARRAY(1) is larger than ARRAY(2) in the original position, the IF statement will go to statement ____10____ the first time it is executed.

2.124 Notice the sequence at statement 10 in this example. A special variable (TEMP) is used to save one of the values when the swap is made. This is necessary because if one value were placed in the other's position *without* first preserving its original value, that original value would be erased and lost forever.

This program could be used to sort an array of any length by defining a different value of the variable (name) ____N____ .

2.125 So far in Part 2, you have been introduced to four of the control statements in the FORTRAN language: the IF statement which provides three possible branch directions based on the value of an expression; the GO TO statement which directs the computer unconditionally to a particular part of the program; the DO statement which controls looping; and the CONTINUE statement which serves the DO statement with a reference point when the loop might otherwise end with a control statement. These four statements are the most important of the control statements, and are required in most programs much more often than the other control statements.

EXERCISE 2.7

Write a program to compute all the possible products of the A and B arrays, each of which contains 20 numbers, placing these products in an array called C (which must hold 400 numbers). Use two nested DO-loops such that C(1) through C(20) contain the products of A(1) times B(1) through B(20), C(21) through C(40) contain the products of A(2) times B(1) through B(20), etc.

2.126 The rest of this chapter will be devoted to the remaining control statements, with particular emphasis on those which apply to the 704/709/7090 version of FORTRAN. In cases where these statements are not allowed or where their use is permitted with restrictions in other FORTRAN systems, a summary frame will be included listing such exception.

2.127 One group of control statements performs the function of testing indicators and switches in the computer itself. These statements choose one of two alternative paths in the program depending on the *on* or *off* condition of the switch or indicator. This provides the programmer with another means of control.

2.128 These two-way branching statements all have the same format: IF (some pertinent word code) x, x where the x's are statement numbers corresponding to the options desired for the condition of *on* and *off,* respectively.

In the control statements which test indicators the *first* statement number option corresponds to the condition of the indicator being _____ on _____ .

2.129 Notice that these two-way branching statements have a different format than the conventional IF statement. The information following the word IF is not a mathematical expression as in the conventional case, but a particular sequence of words which identify the type of statement being used. Also, there are only two branch options in these statements instead of the three with the conventional IF statement.

2.130 There are six independent switches on the console of the 7090 computer. These are called "sense switches" and they may be turned on or off as desired by the computer operator during execution of the program. (The 1620, 7070/7074, 704, 705, and 709 computers also have sense switches.)

2.131 The sense switches may be tested individually by the FORTRAN statement: IF (SENSE SWITCH i) x, x where i is the number corresponding to a particular switch and the x's are statement numbers. The computer will go next to the first of these indicated statements if the switch is *on* or to the second of these statements if the switch is *off*.

The statement IF (SENSE SWITCH 5)10,20 will direct the computer to statement _____ 20 _____ if switch 5 is *off*.

2.132 The sense-switch-testing statement must conform to this exact format: the word IF, an open parenthesis, the words SENSE SWITCH, a switch number, a closing parenthesis, and the two statement numbers separated by a comma. On the 7090 computer, the switch number may be 1, 2, 3, 4, 5, or 6.

[true or false] The statement IF (SENSE SWITCH 6),10,35 is a legal 7090 FORTRAN statement. _____ F _____

2.133 This type of testing statement is used whenever it is necessary to exercise external control over the program. The program can have alternative sequences of statements built in which are selected manually by flipping the appropriate switch. The use of these switches is usually discouraged, however, in favor of other methods of external control.

2.134   Sample program segment:

$$\text{IF (SENSE SWITCH 1)10,30}$$
$$10 \quad \text{IF (SENSE SWITCH 2)20,30}$$
$$20 \quad \text{(Some sequence of statements)}$$
$$\cdots \quad \cdots\cdots\cdots\cdots\cdots\cdots\cdots\cdots\cdots$$
$$30 \quad \text{(Some sequence of statements)}$$

2.135   The sample program segment above shows a case where the computer tests two switches, going to statement 20 if, and only if, both switches are on, and going to statement 30 if either switch is off.

[true or false] In this example, if sense switch 1 is off, the computer will never execute statement 10. _____T_____

---

true

2.136   Most larger computer systems involve closed-shop or automatic operation procedures. Therefore the use of sense switches is usually forbidden. They are included in this manual, as are other features not in popular use, to give a complete picture of the FORTRAN language.

EXERCISE 2.8

Write a DO-loop to do the following:

(a)   If sense switch 1 is *on,* place the entire contents of the A array in the B array.
(b)   If sense switch 1 is *off,* place the entire contents of the A array in the C array.
(c)   In either case, place the sum of all the numbers in the A array in a variable called SUM.

The A array contains 10000 (ten thousand) numbers.

2.137   The 7090 computer has four so-called "sense lights." These lights are displayed on the console and their condition of on or off may be tested by the statement IF (SENSE LIGHT i) x, x where i is a number corresponding to a particular light and the x's are statement numbers with the usual meaning.

The statement IF (SENSE LIGHT 4)1,2 tests the condition of light number _____4_____ .

4

2.138   As was the case with the other testing statements, the options in the sense-light-testing statement correspond to the conditions of *on* and *off* respectively. If the light is on, the first indicated statement is taken next and the light is

71

turned off. If the light is originally off, it remains that way and the second statement is selected.

Regardless of the condition of the light before a sense-light-testing statement, the light will be (on or off) ___*off*___ after execution of such a statement.

off

2.139   The sense lights can be turned on or off only by the computer. The FORTRAN statement to turn the lights on is SENSE LIGHT *i* where the *i* is a sense light number (1, 2, 3, or 4 on the 7090). The same statement with zero for the *i* will turn *all* the lights *off*.

The statements SENSE LIGHT 1, IF (SENSE LIGHT 1)10,20 executed in that order will take the computer to statement ___10___.

10

2.140   The sense lights and their testing statements are used where it is possible for the program itself to dictate a future branching condition. Like the sense switch statement, their use is not too common.

2.141   To summarize, the control statements covered so far in this chapter are:

Name	Example
IF	IF (EXAMPL)100,200,10
GO TO	GO TO 1000
DO	DO 55 K = 1,1000
CONTINUE	CONTINUE
IF (SENSE SWITCH)	IF (SENSE SWITCH 5)10,20
IF (SENSE LIGHT)	IF (SENSE LIGHT 1)101,102
SENSE LIGHT	SENSE LIGHT 3

2.142   The 7090 computer has some indicators which will warn of possible error conditions. These conditions are overflow and division by zero. If you understand the meaning of overflow you may skip the next frame.

2.143   Overflow is the condition which occurs when a number becomes too large for the computer to handle owing to some mathematical operation. You have probably seen a desk calculator with the adder register full of 9s, and when 1 is added to this quantity—zip! All the digits go to zero with an imaginary 1 overflowing to the left. This is exactly equivalent to overflow in the computer.

2.144   Consider a fictitious computer with room enough for a five-digit number. The largest number this computer can handle is 99999. Suppose that value (99999) has the quantity 10 added to it as the result of a programmed operation—the result would be 100009. Our computer can only hold the lower five digits, 00009.

This computer would try to tell you that your answer was 00009, which is not correct. This situation may occur on any computer which has a limit to the size of number it can handle (limit on the 7090: approximately 10^{38}).

2.145 On the 7090 computer if overflow occurs due to addition or multiplication, an indicator called "accumulator overflow" is turned on. If the overflow is due to division, an indicator called "quotient overflow" is turned on. The statements to test these conditions are explained in the next frame.

If overflow occurred in our fictitious computer from adding 80000 to 50000, the incorrect result would be ___30000___ .

30000

2.146 The condition of accumulator overflow is tested by the statement IF ACCUMULATOR OVERFLOW x, x; quotient overflow is tested by the statement IF QUOTIENT OVERFLOW x, x. In both cases the x's are statement numbers corresponding to options for the condition of the indicator being *on* or *off*, respectively.

If you suspect overflow due to division, you may tell the computer to go next to statement 1 if overflow has occurred, or to statement 2 if it has not, by the statement: ___IF QUOTIENT OVERFLOW 1, 2___

IF QUOTIENT OVERFLOW 1,2

2.147 Notice that these two statements, unlike the sense light and sense switch statements, require no parentheses. This is important to note since the statement is incorrect unless worded exactly as indicated. Like the sense light statement, however, either overflow indicator is turned off when tested.

The overflow-testing statements comprise ___2___-way branches.

---

two

2.148 A serious error condition can exist if you accidentally try to tell the computer to divide by the quantity *zero*. When this is attempted, the division does not take place and the indicator called "divide check" is turned on. The program, however, goes merrily on its way as if the division had been done correctly, unless detected.

The divide check indicator is turned on when an attempt is made to divide by ___0___ .

---

zero

2.149 The statement IF DIVIDE CHECK x, x will test the condition of the divide check indicator, going to the first indicated statement number if the indi-

73

cator is *on* or to the second statement if the indicator is *off*. If the indicator is on, it is turned off by this statement.

The statement sequence A = 0.0 C = B/A IF DIVIDE CHECK 40,41 will direct the computer to statement ____40____ .

2.150   Remember, the conditions of quotient overflow and divide check are not the same; the quotient overflow condition occurs when the result of any division is larger than the computer can handle (greater than 10^{38} on the 7090, for example). The divide check condition occurs only when you attempt to divide by *zero*.

[true or false] When divide check condition occurs, usually by accident, the numerical results are meaningless because the divide operation does not take place. ____T____

2.151   The three statements IF ACCUMULATOR OVERFLOW, IF QUO-TIENT OVERFLOW, and IF DIVIDE CHECK may be used on the 705, 7070/7074, or 704/709/7090 computers. The 1620 and 650 FORTRAN versions do not permit these statements. (NOTE: unlike the SENSE-type tests, parentheses are not allowed in the above-mentioned statements.)

Assume that both overflow indicators are *off* and the divide check indicator is *on;* what statement will the computer execute after completing this sequence? ____60____

          10   IF ACCUMULATOR OVERFLOW 40,20
          20   IF QUOTIENT OVERFLOW 50,30
          30   IF DIVIDE CHECK 60,40

2.152   This was a fairly simple program trace. Remember the conditions of the problem; both overflow indicators are *off,* the divide check indicator is *on.* Look again at the three statements.

          10   IF ACCUMULATOR OVERFLOW 40,20
          20   IF QUOTIENT OVERFLOW 50,30
          30   IF DIVIDE CHECK 60,40

The first statement will direct the computer to statement 20 because the indicator is *off*. Statement 20 happens to be the next statement in the list.

When statement 20 (IF QUOTIENT OVERFLOW 50,30) is executed, since the quotient overflow is given to be *off,* the computer will go next to statement _____ .

2.153 Statement 30 of this example (30   IF DIVIDE CHECK 60,40) tests the divide check indicator. Since this was given as being *on,* the final branch (your answer) could be only one possible choice, statement 60.

When statement 60 is being executed, all three indicators are in the _____ condition.

2.154 If you answered this question correctly and if you feel that you understand this material thoroughly, you may go on to the next frame. If you feel in need of review, go back to frame 2.142 and read over this material again.

2.155 The list of control statements is growing:

IF	IF (SENSE SWITCH i)	IF ACCUMULATOR OVERFLOW
GO TO	IF (SENSE LIGHT i)	IF QUOTIENT OVERFLOW
DO	SENSE LIGHT i	IF DIVIDE CHECK
CONTINUE		

2.156 The next three control statements are used for the purpose of multiple-path branching. The IF statement, you will recall, has *three* possible branch directions, and the indicator-testing statements have exactly *two* alternatives. The next few frames will explain the statements used for multiple-path branching.

2.157 The first of the multiple-branching statements is a special form of the GO TO statement called the "computed GO TO" statement. It begins with the words "GO TO" followed by a pair of parentheses containing any desired amount of statement numbers separated by commas. The closing parenthesis is followed by a comma and a nonsubscripted *fixed-point* variable. An example of a computed GO TO is shown below:

GO TO (10,9,8,7,6,5,4,3,2,1), N

2.158 As in most control statements, the format is most important, so let's go over it once more: the words GO TO, an open parenthesis, a series of statement numbers separated by commas, a closing parenthesis, a comma, and, lastly, a fixed-point variable. Each of these items must be present.

[true or false] The statement GO TO (1,2,10)I is a legal computed GO TO statement. ___E___

> false
>
> A comma *must* be used to separate the closing parenthesis and the variable.

2.159   The computed GO TO is executed as follows: the computer will go next to the statement whose statement number appears in the parenthesized list in the order corresponding to the value of the fixed-point variable. That is, if the variable has a value of 1 the *first* number in the list is the next statement; if the value is 2 the *second* statement number is the next statement, and so on.

In the statement GO TO (10,9,8,7,6,5,4,3,2,1),N if N has a value of 3 the computer will go next to statement ___6___ .

> 8

2.160   The variable's value does not have a direct bearing on the statement *number* chosen for the next statement to be executed. For example, in the statement GO TO (10,9,8,7,6,5,4,3,2,1),N a value of 10 for the variable N will *not* direct the computer to statement 10. Rather, N acts like a subscript to the list of numbers.

In the example shown above, a value of 10 for the variable N will direct the computer to statement ___1___ .

> 1

2.161   The list of statement numbers may be as long as desired and the same number may appear more than once in the list if desired (as was permitted in IF statements). Care must be taken to see that the control variable on the right does not have a value larger than the number of statement numbers in the list.

In the statement GO TO (312,311,312,1),K the value of K must never exceed (number) ___4___ .

> 4

2.162   The computed GO TO is available in all FORTRAN systems. It is used whenever it is convenient for the computer to select one of several branch options through the value of a variable. Suppose, for example, that you wish to go to different parts of the program depending on the value of a variable X which has a value between 0. and 10. If the value is between 0. and 1.0 (including 0. but not the upper bound) you wish to go to statement 1; if the value is between 1.0 and 2.0, you wish to go to 2, etc.

2.163   Sample program segment:

$$K = X + 1.0$$
$$GO\ TO\ (1,2,3,4,5,6,7,8,9,10,10),\ K$$

2.164   The above program uses the value of the tested variable X to form a control variable K. In a floating-point expression the variable X has 1.0 added to it, then this value is converted to fixed-point (integer) mode and placed in K. If X had a value between 0. and 1.0, K would have a value of 1; for X between 1. and 2., K would be 2, etc.

[true or false] K will always have an integer value due to the truncation of fractions in fixed-point numbers. _____T_____

true

2.165   This computed GO TO (frame 2.163) lists the options from which the computer chooses, depending on the value of the control variable K. Remember, K's value depends on the value of X. When the GO TO is executed, the statement selected will indirectly depend on the value of X as outlined in the problem statement.

Looking at the sample program segment in frame 2.163, if the value of X were exactly 10.0, what statement would the computer choose (K would be 11)? __10__

10

EXERCISE 2.9

Write the first two statements of a DO-loop which will cycle ten times and execute statement 10 on the first pass; 20, the second pass; 30, the third pass; etc.

2.166   There is a statement type called the assigned GO TO which is similar to the computed GO TO in format and usage. The assigned GO TO is employed in situations where the branch point directions can be preset in the program, rather than being dependent on some computed quantity as the computed GO TO is.

2.167   The assigned GO TO statement has a format similar to the computed GO TO. The statement begins with the words GO TO followed by a fixed-point variable name and followed in turn by a comma and a pair of parentheses containing a list of statement numbers. (Example: GO TO N, (41,57,19).

Like the computed GO TO statement, the statement numbers in an assigned GO TO must be separated by ___Comma___.

commas

2.168   When an assigned GO TO statement is executed the computer will go next to one of the statements whose numbers are included in the parenthesized list. The choice is made according to the statement number which is currently "assigned" to the fixed-point variable name in the statement. The procedure for assigning such a statement number is explained in the next frame.

If statement 101 is assigned to the variable KOUNT, the computer will go next to statement _____ 101 _____ when executing the statement GO TO KOUNT, (1,2,3,101,55).

> 101

2.169   The assignment of a statement number to the fixed-point variable is done by the ASSIGN statement. This statement consists of the word ASSIGN followed by a statement number, the word TO, and the variable name to which the number is to be assigned. (Example: ASSIGN 101 TO KOUNT.)

The sequence ASSIGN 589 TO INDEX, GO TO INDEX, (5,10,55,587,589), executed in that order, will tell the computer to go next to statement _____ 589 _____.

> 589

2.170   Notice that the name KOUNT was used in the example of frame 2.168. This is an example of adapting a variable name to suit the mode required in a particular application. For example, the statement GO TO COUNT, (12,43,55) would not be valid because the control variable must be fixed-point.

If you wished to assign the statement 10 to the variable NIGHT you would write _____ ASSIGN 10 TO NIGHT _____

> ASSIGN 10 TO NIGHT

2.171   Incidentally, the use of the ASSIGN statement is quite different from the operation of setting a variable *equal to* a quantity in an arithmetic formula statement. The ASSIGN statement is used only in conjunction with an assigned GO TO; the use of an arithmetic formula to set a variable equal to a statement number will not work.

When an assigned GO TO statement is executed, the fixed-point variable in the statement must have had a statement number _____ ASSIGNED _____ to it.

> assigned

2.172   The statement number list in an assigned GO TO statement must include all possible statement numbers which might be assigned to the variable. Conversely, the program should not assign a statement number which is not in the list of any assigned GO TO using that variable.

[true or false] The statements ASSIGN 10 TO NUMBER and NUMBER = 10 are equivalent. ___F___

false
Assigning a number to a variable is different from setting that variable equal to a number.

2.173   One other important note: a variable to which statement numbers are assigned should not be used as a conventional variable in the same program. The operation of "assigning" a statement number is a very special operation and should not be mixed with the ordinary use of variables.

The statement GO TO (8,7,6,5), K is a _computed_ GO TO type, while the statement GO TO K, (8,7,6,5), is a _assigned_ GO TO statement.

computed, assigned

2.174   The assigned GO TO statement is used where it is possible for the program itself to preset the branch direction at a branch point. In such case, the branch direction depends on which prior path the computer had taken through the program (and consequently which ASSIGN statement had been executed previously).

[true or false] The sequence ASSIGN 55 TO K. . . . GO TO K, (1,2,5,3,100) is legal. ___F___

false
A statement number is assigned which is not in the ensuing GO TO list.

2.175   Many cases arise in which it appears offhand that either the assigned or the computed GO TO statement is applicable. In such cases, use the assigned GO TO since it is slightly more efficient than the computed GO TO. The illustration in the next frame shows a case where it is definitely preferable to use the assigned GO TO form.

2.176 Sample program segment:

```
         IF (A − B)10,20,30
    10   ASSIGN 100 TO N
         (Some statement sequence)
         GO TO 50
    20   ASSIGN 200 TO N
         (Some statement sequence)
         GO TO 50
    30   ASSIGN 300 TO N
         (Some statement sequence)
    50   (Some common statement sequence)
         GO TO N, (100,200,300)
   . . .   . . . . . . . . . . . . . . . . . . . . . . . . . . . . . . . .
   100   (Some statement sequence)
   200   (Some statement sequence)
   300   (Some statement sequence)
```

2.177 In the sample program segment above, the ASSIGN statement is used to preset the branch point options according to whether the IF statement directs the computer to statement numbers 10, 20, or 30. In this case, the numbers 100, 200, or 300 would be assigned, respectively. Thus, when the assigned GO TO statement is executed, it will select its branch according to where the computer had been before. Incidentally, this is faster on the computer than using the statement IF (A − B)100,200,300 at that point.

2.178 The assigned GO TO form is available in the following FORTRAN systems: 705, 7070/7074, 704, 709, and 7090. This statement (and, of course, the ASSIGN statement) cannot be used with the 650 and 1620 FORTRAN systems.

2.179 The following is a list of the control statements described so far in this chapter:

IF	IF ACCUMULATOR OVERFLOW
GO TO	IF QUOTIENT OVERFLOW
DO	IF DIVIDE CHECK
CONTINUE	Computed GO TO
IF (SENSE SWITCH *i*)	Assigned GO TO
IF (SENSE LIGHT *i*)	ASSIGN
SENSE LIGHT *i*	

2.180 The next two control statements are used to bring the computer to a halt. As such they do not quite fit the general definition of control statements (telling the computer where to go next) but they do exercise some "control" in their execution.

2.181   The first of the halting control statements is the STOP statement. This consists very simply of the word STOP, and its execution is exactly what the name implies. The computer is brought to a halt and may not be restarted without beginning all over again. For example:

> (Your program statements)
> STOP

Simple enough?

2.182   A similar statement which will also cause the computer to halt is the PAUSE statement, which consists of the word PAUSE. When the PAUSE statement is executed, the computer will halt, but if the START button on the computer console is pushed, the computer will continue on in the program at the statement following the PAUSE.

The STOP and PAUSE statements both cause the computer to halt but the _____PAUSE_____ statement will permit the computer to start up again when the appropriate button is pushed.

> PAUSE

2.183   In the 7090 FORTRAN system both the STOP and PAUSE statements may be followed by a number of up to five digits which will be displayed on the computer console lights when the halt occurs. This is helpful in identifying which halt occurred in a program that has several such halts. One catch: this code number must contain digits between 0 and 7 (octal digits) in the 7090 computer. An example is shown below:

> 100   (Some sequence of statements)
> PAUSE 77777
> GO TO 100

EXERCISE 2.10

Perform the division of corresponding numbers in the A and B arrays (i.e. A(1)/B(1), A(2)/B(2), etc.), placing each quotient in corresponding order in the C array. If overflow occurs, do a computer halt with a 1 displayed on the console; if a divide check occurs, halt the computer with a 2 displayed. In either case, tell the computer to continue the loop when the START button is pushed. The arrays contain 1500 numbers each. NOTE: Both conditions (overflow and divide check) cannot occur simultaneously.

2.184   Actually the STOP and PAUSE statements are not often used in the larger computers such as the 7090. These systems are usually governed by a monitor program and a special statement is used in place of the STOP. This procedure for the 7090 will be explained in a later chapter.

2.185   The basic STOP and PAUSE statements are available on all FORTRAN systems. Check the appropriate manual to verify the use of the code number in a particular system, since this is not permitted on all systems.

2.186   The last statement type covered in this chapter is the END statement. This statement is different from all the other statements covered so far in this course; it is not "executed," but rather acts as a source of information to the program, and as such is actually a specification statement. Its function is very simple: it marks the *last statement* in the written program.

2.187   The END statement is used in all systems except the 705 FORTRAN system. It consists basically of the word END, which may stand alone or be followed by optional information. For the purposes of this course, the form of this statement consisting only of the word END will be discussed.

2.188   As pointed out in the previous frame the only function of the END statement is to mark the last written statement in a program. That is, it has nothing whatever to do with halting the computer or any other "executable" operation. All programs written in FORTRAN are incomplete until an END statement is appended to the "end" of the list of statements.

This completes the discussion of control statements. You may proceed to the examination on the next page, after which you may go on to Part 3.

PART 2: EXAMINATION

1. Given the following conditions in the 7090 computer:

$X = -22.5$ N assigned statement number 300
$Y = +16.9$ Accumulator overflow indicator *on*
$Z = +5.6$ Quotient overflow indicator *off*
$I = 3$ Sense switch 3 *on*, all others *off*
                 Sense lights 1 and 3 *on*, others *off*

indicate the statement number to be executed next after each of the following statements.

(a) IF (X)20,30,40: __20__
(b) IF ACCUMULATOR OVERFLOW 50,60: __50__
(c) GO TO 101: __101__
(d) GO TO N, (299,300,301): __300__
(e) IF (X + Y + Z)11,12,13: __12__
(f) IF (SENSE SWITCH 6)31,32: __32__
(g) GO TO (11,12,13,14), I: __3__ _?
(h) IF QUOTIENT OVERFLOW 18,20: __20__
(i) IF (I − 1)16,26,36: __36__
(j) IF (SENSE LIGHT 1)1000,1001: __1000__

2. Indicate which 7090 FORTRAN statements below have "bugs" and point out each error (there is no more than one per statement).

(a) IF (X ** 2 − 1.0), 1,1,2: ___)___
(b) GO TO SLEEP, (1,2,3): _____
(c) STOP 99: _____
(d) ASSIGN 20 TO X: _____
(e) DO 30 INDEX = 5, J: _____
(f) IF (SENSE LIGHT 6)10,11: _____
(g) IF (NUMBER)10,20,30,40: _____
(h) GO TO MORROW, (8,18): _____
(i) A(K) = X(1) + Y(A): _____
(j) PAWS 77777: _____

3. Write a program to compute the square roots of the floating-point whole numbers ranging from 1.0 to 100.0 and place these roots in the 100-number array called ROOT.

4. Assume that the program shown below has been completely executed. Indicate the number of times each statement will have been executed.

Line	Statement	Count
5	X = 0.0	1
10	DO 500 I = 1, 100	100
50	X = X + 1.0	100
55	IF (X − 20.0)101,101,100	100
100	IF (X − 80.0)102,102,103	80
101	A(I) = 3.0 * X ** 2 + 4.0 * X	20
75	GO TO 500	20
102	A(I) = 5.0 * X ** 2 + 6.0 * X	60
76	GO TO 500	60
103	A(I) = 7.0 * X ** 2 + 8.0 * X	20
500	CONTINUE	100
1000	STOP	1

5. Given an array called A containing 1000 numbers, write a program to compute the polynomial $4a_i^4 - 3a_i^3 + 2a_i^2 - 16$ for all values of the A array. If the polynomial value is positive or zero, place that number in the array called XPOS in the next available position; if the computed value is negative place it in similar fashion in an array called XNEG.

PART 3

INPUT AND OUTPUT
STATEMENTS

You have been shown how to construct the middle part of a computer program—the part in which you tell the computer how to manipulate the numbers and also how to make simple tests and decisions from which it executes control. Most programs require that the computer also be able to accept information at the start of the program and to divulge the results at the conclusion. In other words, the computer must be capable of "readin' and writin' " as well as " 'rithmetic." Various computer systems use different media for these operations of input and output; most commonly, the input information comes from punched cards, punched tape, or magnetic tape, while output data is usually written on a printer or magnetic tape or, less commonly, punched on cards or paper tape. The 7090, for example, has a card reader, card punch, printer, and several magnetic tapes in a typical system.

This chapter will discuss the input/output statements used by the FORTRAN language, primarily oriented to the 704/709/7090 family but with pertinent comments on other systems, as in the preceding chapter.

3.1 It is important that a computer be able to accept information from external sources. Today's computers are built to "read" information in a variety of ways from several kinds of equipment. The basic 7090 can, for example, accept information from punched cards or magnetic tape.

3.2 Since the computer can read information while the program is running, a general problem solution can be programmed such that the actual numbers to be used will be supplied each time the program is run. In this fashion, the program can be re-used as often as desired, with only the numbers involved being changed.

[true or false] A computer can supply the numbers to be used in a program by "reading" them from punched cards, magnetic tape, and similar sources. _____ .

true

3.3 In the FORTRAN language the *input statements* are used to define the value of a variable or list of variables. These variables are used by name in appropriate statements later in the program with the understanding that their values will be supplied at the time the program is run.

Variables may have their values defined either by arithmetic formula statements or by _____ statements.

input

3.4 Of course, you could define all the variables used in a program with arithmetic formula statements, perhaps by setting them equal to constants. However, each time you executed the program, the results would be the same. The whole point of using input statements is to gain the flexibility of changing the values of the quantities used by the program.

3.5 Sample program segment:

$$A = 3.0$$
$$B = 2.5$$
$$C = 1.0$$
$$40 \quad Y = A * X ** 2 + B * X + C$$

3.6 In the sample program segment shown above, the quantities A, B, and C are defined by equating them to constants. Wherever the variables A, B, and C are used in the program they will have these given values, and, moreover, every time the program is run they will have those values!

When statement 40 in the above segment is executed the value of the variable A will always be _____ .

3.7 In the above example, the variables A, B, and C are defined by setting them equal to constants in arithmetic formula statements. Those three statements might be replaced by the statement

$$\text{READ } 1,A,B,C$$

and followed by $\qquad Y = A * X ** 2 + B * X + C$

[true or false] All three variables, A, B, and C, have their values defined in a single statement in the example above. _____

3.8 The statement READ 1,A,B,C is an example of a FORTRAN input statement. This statement means that the computer will read three values from the *card reader* and assign them to the variables A, B, and C respectively.

Write a similar READ statement to define the variables X, Y, and Z.

_____

3.9 The READ statement is constructed as follows: the word READ, a statement number, and a list of variables, each of which is preceded by a comma. The statement number refers to an associated statement whose meaning is explained later. (In our examples the number 1 will be used unless otherwise requested.)

The statement READ 1, WORD will define the value of the variable _____ .

3.10   The list of variables following the statement number in the READ statement may be of any desired length. For example, READ 1,A,B,C,D,E,F,G,H,-O,P,Q,R,S,T,U,V,W,X,Y,Z will read twenty values from the card reader and assign them to the respective variables.

[true or false] The READ statement reads values from the card reader only.
_____

true

3.11   Incidentally, the variables in the list of a READ statement may be of either mode. Moreover, both fixed-point and floating-point variable values may be specified in the same list with no taboo about mixing the modes.

[true or false] According to the above definition, the statement READ 1,A,B,C, I,J,K is not valid. _____

false
It is perfectly valid.

3.12   The variables in the READ statement list may or may not be sub-scripted as desired. The subscripts, if used, may be constants or previously defined variables, and even the accepted form of subscript expression is permitted. For example, the statement READ 1,A,B,X(3),N(K) will read four numbers from the card reader, assigning the values respectively to A,B, the third number in the X array, and the Kth number in the N array.

[true or false] The statement READ 1,A($2 * K - 5$) is a valid READ statement.
_____

true

3.13   The significant points covered so far have been: the computer can read data at the time the program is being run, reading from a variety of media; the READ statement causes the computer to read punched cards in the attached card reader; the READ statement contains a list of variables which specifies where the numbers being read are to be assigned; the variables in the list may be of either mode and may contain subscripts.

Write a statement to read (from cards) a value for each of the variables ALPHA, BETA, and GAMMA, in that order.

READ 1, ALPHA, BETA, GAMMA
    If your answer agrees exactly with the one shown above, do Exercise 3.1. If you have omitted any of the three commas, take note of where they belong. If your answer was otherwise wrong, go on to frame 3.14.

3.14   The answer should have been pretty obvious; a READ statement was called for, starting with the word READ and the statement number (which we said would be 1 for our examples).

The first two parts of the requested statement should be _____
_____ .

READ 1

3.15   The rest of the statement consists of the list of variables to be defined: ALPHA, BETA, and GAMMA. Each name must be preceded by a comma.

The complete statement to read values for the variables JOE, JIM, and JACK would be: _____ .

READ 1, JOE, JIM, JACK
    If you answered this satisfactorily, do Exercise 3.1; if not, go back to frame 3.3 and review this material.

EXERCISE 3.1

Write a statement to read ten numbers from a card and place them in the variables A, B, C, D, E, F, G, H, O, and P, respectively. Use associated statement 1 in the READ statement.

3.16   The associated statement whose number appears in a READ statement plays an important part in the reading operation. This statement is called a FORMAT statement and its job is to tell the computer how the numbers being read are laid out on the cards (which columns are punched, how many per card, etc.).

The statement READ 10,A,B,C refers to FORMAT statement number _____ .

10

3.17   Nearly all input statements use a FORMAT statement to specify the way the numbers are laid out in the cards, magnetic tape, or other external medium. The general rule is that the input statement tells the computer *what* is to be read and the FORMAT specifies *how* and *where* the numbers will be found.

[yes or no] Does the statement READ 1,A,B,C tell you how many *cards* are to be read? _____

no

3.18   Almost all input statements contain a *list* of variables which specifies the quantities being read. The next few frames will explain a few details of how the list is used.

3.19 When an input statement such as a READ statement is executed, the values being read are immediately defined as the values of their corresponding variables in the list. Thus, a fixed-point value read early in the list can be used as a subscript later in the list (e.g., READ 1,K,(A(K))).

3.20 When the statement READ 1, K, (A(K)) is executed, two numbers will be read from a card. The first number, a fixed-point quantity, will become the subscript of the second number immediately. In this fashion a deck of cards can be indexed and need not be sorted into any special order.

If the value of K on a particular card is read as 3, the second number on that card will be assigned to the _____ number of the A array, using the statement shown above.

third

3.21 When this feature of using a read-in value as a subscript in the same list is employed, a special restriction must be observed; at least one open parenthesis (other than the normal subscript parentheses) must separate the two references to that fixed-point variable, as in READ 1, K, (A(K)). Naturally, it must also be balanced with a closing parenthesis.

The statement READ 1,I,J,K,(A(I),B(J),C(K)) will cause a total of _____ values to be read.

six

3.22 When variables appear in an input list with variable subscripts, these subscripts need not necessarily be defined within the same list as in the preceding example. Their subscript values may have been defined by other statements (by a DO-loop index, for example).

3.23 Sample program segment:

$$4 \quad DO \ 5 \ I = 1,10$$
$$5 \quad READ \ 1,A(I)$$

3.24 The sample program segment shows a read statement which will be executed a total of ten times. Each time it is executed a value will be read and placed in the A array, its position determined by the DO index value.

In the sample program of frame 3.23, the sixth time that statement 5 is executed, a value will be assigned to A(_____). (Fill in a number.)

6

3.25 You now have seen two examples of subscripted variables in an input statement list. The first example showed the subscript value being defined within the same list; the second example showed another means of defining that subscript's value (notice, no extra parentheses required in this second case). One more example similar to the second case will be shown in the next frame.

3.26   Sample program segment:

$$\text{READ 1, N}$$
$$\text{DO 5 I = 1, N}$$
$$\text{5   READ 1, A(I)}$$

The first READ statement in the example above causes the computer to read a single quantity, N, which then becomes the upper limit of a DO-loop. Thus, the read-in value of N determines the amount of numbers which will be read within the DO-loop itself.

If the value read for N were 50, statement 5 above would be executed a total of _____ times.

50

3.27   An input statement's list of variables may have subscripts which are also variables. As shown in the preceding examples, these variable subscripts may have their values defined either by reading them in the same list, or by other statements preceding the READ statement (by a DO-loop, for example).

EXAMPLE 3.2

Given 100 cards containing 3 numbers each, write a program to read each card and place the three numbers in arrays A, B, and C, respectively, in the order read (first three to A(1), B(1), C(1); next three to A(2), B(2), etc.).

3.28   A DO-loop, then, is one method for programming the reading of arrays. Another method, more widely used, is the *self-indexing* list technique. In this type of input statement list, the variables with their variable subscripts are followed by an *index definition* exactly as defined in a DO-loop. For instance:

$$\text{READ 1,(A(I),I = 1,50)}$$

3.29   The statement READ 1,(A(I),I = 1,50) is identical in operation to the statement READ 1,A(1),A(2),A(3),A(4), . . . ,A(50). This statement, though executed only once, will cause the reading of 50 numbers into successive positions in the A array.

The statement READ 1,(ARRAY(K),K = 1,1000) will cause a total of _____ numbers to be read.

1000

3.30   The index definition as used in input lists may utilize the same features available to DO-loops. It may have variables for lower or upper limits and it may use the optional third quantity defining an increment other than one (which may also be a variable if desired).

3.31   Take the statement READ 1, N,(A(I), I = 2, N) for example. In this statement, the index definition contains a variable as the upper limit; the value of this variable is read in the same list. The execution of this statement is to read a fixed-point quantity, N, and then read values into A(2) through A(N), inclusive.

If the first number punched in the first card read by the above statement were 15, a total of _____ values would then be read into the A array.

3.32   This self-indexing input list is a very useful shorthand method of reading long lists of quantities. You can well imagine the cumbersome list that would result if you read in a large amount of numbers by naming each one in the input list.

If you wished to read 100 numbers into the A array with the statement READ 1,N,(A(I), I = 1, N) the first number on the first card must be punched as _____ (number).

3.33   Like most other FORTRAN statements, the format which you must observe is rather strict; the subscripted variable (or variables) must be separated from the index definition by a comma (and from each other, if more than one). The entire sequence—variables, dummy subscripts, and index definition—must be enclosed in parentheses.

The statement READ 1,A(I), I = 1, 10 is not valid because of the absence of _____ .

3.34   An input list may contain other elements either before or after a self-indexing sequence. For example, the statement

$$\text{READ } 1,A,B,C,(X(I), I = 1, 3),D,E,F$$

is perfectly valid. The nine values read by this statement will be assigned respectively to A, B, C, X(1), X(2), X(3), D, E, and F.

If the upper limit of the index definition in the example shown above were 10 instead of 3, a total of _____ numbers would be read by this statement.

3.35 More than one variable may be included in a self-indexing sequence, as in the statement READ 1,(A(I),B(I), I = 1, 100). This will cause 200 numbers to be read and assigned in the order A(1), B(1), A(2), B(2), A(3), . . . , A(100), B(100).

The *sixth* number read by the statement shown above would be assigned to _____ (variable and subscript).

3.35A An input list may also contain more than one self-indexing sequence, as in the example statement READ 1, (A(I), I = 1, 10), (B(I), I = 1, 10). This will cause the computer to read 20 numbers and assign them in the order A(1), A(2), A(3), . . . , A(10), B(1), B(2), B(3), . . . , B(10).

The number assigned to B(3), as read by the statement shown above, would be the _____ number (in the order read by the computer).

3.36 Notice that each separate self-indexing sequence has its own pair of parentheses. Any self-indexing list sequence must be so enclosed in parentheses, and these parentheses must contain only the variable (or variables) whose subscript is indexed, plus the index definition.

Write a statement to read values for the first five numbers in the BLOCK array, using self-indexing form. _____

3.37 Perhaps a redefinition of the self-indexing form is in order. Begin the list with an open parentheses followed by the array name; attached to this name, in parentheses, is a "dummy" subscript; then follows a comma and an index definition which defines the values which will be taken by the dummy subscript; the list is ended by a closing parenthesis.

3.38 The index definition is exactly the same as that used in a DO statement. If you want the index to cycle through values of 1 to 5, for example, you would use the sequence I = 1, 5. The choice of the dummy name is arbitrary, so if that was the only discrepancy, skip the next three frames.

3.39 The entire list includes the array name, subscripted with the dummy index, followed by the index definition. For this problem (to read values for the first five numbers in BLOCK) the list should be:

$$(BLOCK(I), I = 1, 5)$$

Remember, those two commas are absolutely necessary; don't forget them!

3.40 The entire statement required for that answer, again, was READ 1,(BLOCK(I), I = 1, 5). Try another case similar to that one.

Write a statement to read values for ALPHA, BETA, GAMMA, and the first 12 numbers in the OMEGA array, in that order. _____

> READ 1, ALPHA, BETA, GAMMA, (OMEGA(I), I = 1, 12)
>   If your answer agrees with the one shown above, do Exercise 3.3. If you missed this question, you had better go back to frame 3.28 and read again, carefully, the material on self-indexed lists.

EXERCISE 3.3

Write a single statement to read 200 numbers, placing the first 100 numbers in the X array and the next 100 numbers in the Y array.

3.41 Recent examples showed two methods of reading numbers into two different blocks with one statement. In one case, both variables were controlled by the same index definition; the other case showed two separate self-indexed sequences. In the first case the numbers being read alternated from one block to another, while the second case showed that one block was filled before any numbers were read for the second block.

3.42 READ 1,(X(I), Y(I), I = 1, 1000)
The statement above illustrates the first case with two variables under control of the same index. This approach would be used ideally when the data is apt to be found in *pairs* (such as rectangular coordinates). At least, if you programmed this statement, you would have to arrange the data in alternating order in the cards.

[true or false] The statement shown above will read the first 1000 numbers into the X array. _____

> false
>   Every *other* number will be read into the X array.

3.43 READ 1, (X(I), I = 1, 1000), (Y(I), I = 1, 1000)
This statement shows the other form: two self-indexed sequences used end-to-end. This method would be used where the data would be more easily punched in separate blocks on the cards, perhaps where the arrays are unrelated sets of numbers.

[true or false] The first 1000 numbers read by the statement above would be assigned to the X array. _____

3.44   In any event when a READ statement is written into a program and the program is being run, the data punched on the cards must be in the form and order expected. Usually the READ statement is written first and the cards containing the data are punched later, although sometimes the statement is tailored to existing card decks.

[true or false] If a card deck exists which has consecutive pairs of x and y coordinates (100 pairs in all) a statement such as READ 1, (X(I), Y(I), I = 1, 100) should be used to read this deck. _____

3.45   You might question the usefulness of the self-indexing technique, since a DO statement could conceivably perform the same function. For example, the sequence DO 10 I = 1, 1000, 10 READ 1, X(I) would admittedly perform the same operation as READ 1, (X(I), I = 1, 1000). There is a reason, however.

The first example above would execute the READ statement _____ time(s) and the second example would execute the READ statement _____ time(s).

3.46   There is one slight difference, as pointed out by the last question and the answer shown above; the DO-loop must necessarily execute the READ statement 1000 times, reading one number each time. The self-indexed version executes the READ only once while cycling its own index and reading the 1000 numbers.

3.47   As the preceding frame points out, there is one slight but important difference in the DO-loop and self-indexed methods: the number of times the READ statement is executed. Herein lies the rub—*each* time a READ statement is executed, a *new card* must be read by the computer!

Using the DO-loop method where the READ statement is executed 1000 times, at least _____ cards will have to be read.

3.48   The DO-loop method executes and reexecutes the READ statement, and each time it does so, a new card must be read. The self-indexing method, on the other hand, depends on the FORMAT statement to indicate how many numbers are punched on each card and, in this way, determines when a new card must be read.

The statement READ 1, (X(I), I = 1, 1000) is executed a total of _____ time(s) to read 1000 numbers.

3.49 Now the advantage of the self-indexing method is becoming clear. The data cards may be utilized much more efficiently if more than one number is allowed per card. For example, if the associated FORMAT statement permits ten numbers per card, only 100 cards would be required to read the 1000 numbers of the preceding example using self-indexed lists, instead of the 1000 cards required with the DO-loop.

3.50 To review, the READ statement causes the computer to start reading a new card in the attached card reader and to read enough cards to supply values for all the variables in the READ statement's list of variables. The list may contain combinations of the following items: nonsubscripted variables, variables with either constant or variable subscripts, or self-indexed sequences with the dummy subscript and index definition.

EXERCISE 3.4

Given a deck of 500 cards containing an integer and four floating-point numbers each, write a loop to read each card and place the four numbers, respectively in the W, X, Y, and Z arrays in the position indicated by the integer read from the card.

3.51 The FORTRAN language has a statement type for reading magnetic tape in a manner similar to that which you have just learned for cards. Many systems have magnetic tapes (all the larger computers and many of the smaller ones with special equipment), and their high speed performance makes them more desirable as input/output units than the much slower card equipment.

3.52 Numbers can be placed on magnetic tape so that they look the same to the computer as they would on cards. In fact the term "card image" will be frequently employed in Part 3, referring to numbers written on magnetic tape in the same format that they would appear on punched cards.

Wherever possible, the use of tapes is recommended over cards for their _____ of operation.

3.53 The numbers can be put on a magnetic tape by a computer (writing) or by a separate card-to-tape copying machine. This latter process places card images, copied directly from punched cards on the tape in coded form.

[true or false] The computer can easily read numbers from magnetic tape because they appear in the same image as punched cards. _____

3.54 On very large computers (where the cost of computer time is very high) large amounts of data recorded on punched cards are copied onto tape for higher speed processing. The FORTRAN statement which controls the reading of tape is essentially the same as the READ statement with slightly different wording, making it very simple to write programs to read tape instead of cards.

Numbers can be copied onto tape directly from _____ .

3.55 The FORTRAN statement to read numbers from magnetic tape is the READ INPUT TAPE statement, consisting of the words READ INPUT TAPE followed by a number, a comma, a statement number, another comma, and an input list, subject to exactly the same rules and restrictions of the READ statement list.

[yes or no] According to the above definition, the statement

$$\text{READ INPUT TAPE 2,10,X,Y,Z}$$

is a valid statement. _____

3.56 The READ INPUT TAPE statement is literally a READ statement with a couple of extra words. The words INPUT TAPE and a tape number (followed by a comma, of course) appear between the word READ and the FORMAT statement number. They operate in similar fashion, too; the computer starts a tape unit in motion and reads numbers for the variables in the list according to the associated FORMAT, just as before.

Change the statement READ 1,A,M,X so that it will read the same information from tape 9. _____

3.57 Let's look at another sample statement, READ INPUT TAPE 12,10,-A,B,C, which will tell the computer to read from tape unit 12, according to FORMAT statement 10, reading a total of three values to be assigned, respectively, to A, B, and C.

Like the READ statement the variables whose values are to be defined are specified in a _____ .

3.58   The list of variables is subject to exactly the same rules as the list of a READ statement. Variables, either with or without subscripts, appear in the list in the order in which their values are to be found on the tape. Self-indexing form may be used.

The statement READ INPUT TAPE 2,2,(A(I), I = 1, 1000) will read a total of _____ values from tape unit 2.

3.59   Actually if you understand READ statements and their lists you automatically understand the READ INPUT TAPE statement; they are virtually identical. Two words and a number represent the absolute difference in their appearance, and their operation is identical except for the medium (cards or tape) selected.

Assuming that our familiar FORMAT number 1 is still with us, write a statement to read in the value of X, Y, Z, XX, YY, and ZZ from tape unit 8.

_____

READ INPUT TAPE 8,1,X,Y,Z,XX,YY,ZZ
   If your answer agrees with the one shown above, skip to frame 3.62. If your answer is wrong continue with frame 3.60.

3.60   Don't make this problem too difficult; it isn't. Given the variables whose values are to be defined (X,Y,Z,XX,YY, and ZZ), and noting that none of them are arrays, makes the list construction a simple matter; just list the variable names in that order.

Write the list only for the problem just completed. _____

X,Y,Z,XX,YY,ZZ
   No parentheses or anything else is required, just the actual list of names.

3.61   Given also that FORMAT number 1 and tape unit 8 are to be used, the construction of the entire statement to solve that problem is now a simple matter of "fill in the blanks" with those numbers.

Write the complete statement. _____

READ INPUT TAPE 8,1,X,Y,Z,XX,YY,ZZ

3.62 Now let's try another similar problem and see how you are making out. Write a statement to read values for ANN, BETTY, CATHY, and the *third* number in the GIRL array, reading from tape 4 with FORMAT 1.

READ INPUT TAPE 4, 1, ANN, BETTY, CATHY, GIRL(3)

3.63 If you are still having difficulty, turn back to frame 3.54 and review the material on tape reading. Otherwise, continue on this page.

Write a statement to read values for M and N which in turn will be the lower and upper index limits respectively, of the BLOCK array which is to be read in the same list. Read from tape 7 with FORMAT 1.

READ INPUT TAPE 7, 1, M, N, (BLOCK(I), I = M, N). All parentheses required.
  If your answer agrees with the one shown (except for possible choice of index variable) do Exercise 3.5 on page 100. If your answer is wrong, continue with the next frame.

3.64 This was a considerably tougher problem than the previous one; you were asked to write a statement to read two numbers (fixed-point) and, using these numbers as the lower and upper index limits respectively, read numerical values for the BLOCK array with self-indexed notation. First of all, the statement begins as usual, READ INPUT TAPE 7, 1, since tape 7 and FORMAT 1 were given.

3.65 It seems the construction of the list for the tape reading statement poses the major problem. First of all, the names M and N must be listed by name (separated by commas), and then the self-indexed list for the BLOCK array follows. This latter element must contain the name, a dummy subscript, and the index definition with M and N used as the lower and upper limits, respectively.

Using I as the dummy subscript and index, write the complete list as requested above: _____ .

M, N, (BLOCK(I), I = M, N)
  The complete statement, of course, is

READ INPUT TAPE 7, 1, M, N, (BLOCK(I), I = M, N)

If you are convinced that you understand the foregoing, continue with Exercise 3.5; otherwise, review some more, starting with frame 3.54.

Tape unit 16 contains 50 fixed-point numbers. Write a statement to read these 50 numbers into the K array in every *other* position (odd-numbered positions) from 1 to 99 inclusive [K(1), K(3), K(5), etc.].

3.66 Considerable mention has been made of the FORMAT statement without defining what it really is. The FORMAT statement is a special type of statement: it is not *executed* in the sense that the other statements are. It falls in a class of statements called "specification" statements. The FORMAT statement, then, is just a reference source for an input (or output) statement. When a READ statement, for example, is being executed, it "consults" the indicated FORMAT statement to find out certain items of information about how the numbers are found on the cards.

When a READ statement needs to know which columns of the card are punched, it consults the _____ .

FORMAT

3.67 Every FORMAT statement is referred to by some input or output statement; consequently, every FORMAT statement has a statement number. The FORMAT statement may be placed anywhere in the program, since it is not executed and has its number for reference (an exception is that it cannot be the first statement after a DO or the last statement of a DO loop).

[yes or no] If a FORMAT has the number 100, is the statement GO TO 100 legal: _____ ?

No
    A FORMAT statement is not executable; therefore, you cannot send the computer to that statement.

3.68 The use of the FORMAT statement is basically simple. Suppose you wish to read six floating-point numbers per card, reading several cards full to fill an array. The FORMAT statement is only concerned with the desired number of values per card and what card columns will contain those numbers. A typical FORMAT which might be used to satisfy the above conditions is FORMAT (6F12.4). The codes are explained later.

[true or false] The FORMAT statement directly defines the number of cards to be read. _____

False
    The FORMAT only specifies how many numbers per card and where they are located on the card.

3.69 Naturally, if you wished to have ten numbers punched per card you would construct the FORMAT statement accordingly. The same is true for any desired card layout you might wish to specify.

If you had a FORMAT specifying six numbers per card and an input statement with a list of 12 variables, using that FORMAT how many cards do you think would be read by the computer? _____

two

3.70 The FORMAT statement is constructed in the following manner: the word FORMAT followed by a pair of parentheses containing the information about the card layout. The contents of these parentheses are explained in the next few frames.

[true or false] The statement 1 FORNAT (card information) is legal as far as shown. _____

False
   FORMAT, like any word in the FORTRAN vocabulary, must be spelled correctly.

3.71 The card layout information contained in the FORMAT statement consists of *number-conversion codes* which tell the computer how many card columns per number, how many decimal places in the number, whether it is fixed-point or floating-point mode, etc. You should distinguish between the terms "number" and "card column." "Number" refers to a complete value, while a "card column" can contain only a single digit.

These number-conversion codes used in FORMAT statements are combinations of alphabetic and numeric characters. The alphabetic characters indicate the desired mode of the number, and the numeric characters tell which card columns are used, etc.

[true or false] The *variable list* in an input (or output) statement defines the card (or card image) layout. _____

False
   The FORMAT statement always specifies these details.

3.72 The number-conversion code for floating-point numbers uses the letter F together with *two* integers separated by a *period* (novelty?) which define, respectively, the number of columns of the card used to contain the number and the position of the decimal point. Example:

$$1 \quad \text{FORMAT (F12.6)}$$

How many card columns do you think the FORMAT above specifies (1,6,12, or 18)? _____

3.73 The example of the previous frame, 1 FORMAT (F12.6), indicates floating-point conversion of a number contained in the first 12 columns of a card (or card image) with 6 decimal places.

FORMAT number-conversion codes use the letter _____ to indicate floating-point conversion.

3.74 The first integer in the FORMAT conversion code specifies the number of card (or card image) columns used to contain the number being read. This item is commonly called the *field width*. When a FORMAT specifies a field width for, say, a card, the number to be read must not exceed the bounds of that field when punched.

The field width specified by the statement 10   FORMAT (F15.2) is _____ columns.

3.75 It should be noted that the *second* integer in the F conversion code—the indicator of the decimal point position—is required in the FORMAT but will be ignored by the computer if an actual decimal point is punched in *any* position in the card being read. If no point is punched, the FORMAT information is used.

The statement 5   FORMAT (F10.1) would specify a total of _____ decimal places if no decimal point were punched on the card.

3.76 Don't confuse the numbers being read from cards with FORTRAN constants; the constant, you will remember, must have a decimal point if it is floating-point. A number being read by the computer with F conversion may have the decimal point omitted and the FORMAT will specify where it belongs.

The statement combination

READ 1,X
1   FORMAT (F15.5)

requires that the number whose value will be read for X be punched in the first _____ columns of the card.

3.77 That first integer in the number-conversion code, which specifies the field width, indicates the *total* column spread occupied by the number. This includes any decimal places specified by the second integer and the column occupied by the decimal point, if punched.

Regardless of the value of the second control integer in a FORMAT conversion code, the total field width depends on the first integer, as in the statement FORMAT (F16.8) which defines a field of _____ columns.

16

3.78 NOTE: the second control integer—the count of the decimal places—must be limited in size. For the 704/709/790 FORTRAN systems, for example, no more than nine decimal-fraction positions are allowed for the F conversion code. If that integer is larger than nine, only the units digit is used (e.g. 16 would be 6).

The statement FORMAT (F20.14) would be treated as if it were written FORMAT (F20. _____).

4

3.79 The element of the FORMAT statement, then, is the number-conversion code. This consists of three items of information in its floating-point form: the mode (indicated by the letter F), the field width (defined by an integer after the F), and the decimal point position (denoted by a second integer, separated from the first with a period).

Write a FORMAT statement to specify converting a floating-point number from the first eight card columns with three decimal places. _____

1   FORMAT (F8.3)
  If your answer agrees exactly with the one shown you are correct and may skip to Exercise 3.6 on page 104. If you did not arrive at the correct answer, continue with the next frame.

3.80 Remember the definition of the number-conversion code? It consists of an alphabetic character to denote the mode, an integer to specify the field width, a period, and a second integer to define decimal point position in case no decimal point is to be included in the number.

[true or false] The statement 1   FORMAT (F12.6) fits the above description.

_____

true

3.81 For floating-point number conversions, the alphabetic code in the FORMAT is F. The two integers used with the F are selected to fit a particular problem; in the preceding diagnostic problem, you were asked to specify eight columns of field width and three decimal places. The complete conversion code for this problem has to be (F8.3).

[yes or no] If you punched a number, *including* its decimal point, on the card to be read by the conversion code shown above, would that integer 3 have any effect?

_____

> no
> This information is only applied when no decimal point is punched in the number being read.

3.82 Let's try another case. Construct a FORMAT statement to specify the conversion of a number (floating-point) contained in the first 15 card columns with a specified number of 7 decimal places. _____

> 1 FORMAT (F15.7)
> If your answer agrees with the one shown above, continue with the next frame. If you still cannot construct a FORMAT statement with the information given, go back to frame 3.66 and review some more.

EXERCISE 3.6

Write a FORMAT statement for each condition described below (all floating-point numbers):

(a) 8 characters, 1 decimal place
(b) 10 characters, 8 decimal places
(c) 6 characters, 2 decimal places
(d) 7 characters, 0 decimal places
(e) 2 characters, 1 decimal place

3.83 If the statement 1 FORMAT (F12.6) were used with the statement READ 1, X, the computer would convert the contents of the first 12 columns of a card into a floating-point number and place that value in the variable X.

Using the same FORMAT, the statement READ 1, Y would define the value of the variable _____.

> Y

3.84 The FORMAT's parentheses contain the complete specification for a card or card image. If there is *one* number-conversion code in a FORMAT this means there will be only *one* number read per card or card image.

How many numeric values *per card* do you think would be indicated by the statement 1 FORMAT (F10.4, F12.6)? _____

3.85 Naturally, then, a FORMAT statement is permitted to have more than one number-conversion code in a single statement. In fact, there is no set limit on the number of conversions permitted in a single FORMAT as long as you stay within the bounds of the card size (72 columns for most cards).

The statement 1 FORMAT (F12.4, F12.6, F6.2) has a total of _____ conversion codes.

3.86 The contents of a FORMAT statement define the layout of a *single* card (or card image). The total column usage of the card is the sum of the field widths of all the number-conversions in the FORMAT. As an example, the statement 1 FORMAT (F12.4, F20.6, F10.5) defines the layout of a card. The first conversion code specifies the contents of columns 1 to 12, the second code specifies columns 13 to 32, and so forth.

The total card usage of the FORMAT shown above is _____ columns.

3.87 So, if you use more than one number-conversion code in a single FORMAT, keep in mind that you are specifying the layout of a card or card image, and be careful that the sum of all the field widths which you specify does not exceed the allowable size of a card. NOTE: naturally, adjacent conversion codes are separated by commas in *all* FORMAT statements.

[true or false] The statement 1 FORMAT (F40.5, F40.5) would be suitable for reading a 72-column card. _____

3.88 In review, the FORMAT statement serves the various input and output statements as a reference or map to specify the condition of the numbers in the external form (how punched on cards, how arranged on tape, etc.). The FORMAT consists of a series of one or more number-conversion codes, each of which specifies the mode, length, and decimal point position of a single number. The entire series of codes constitutes the layout of an entire card or card image.

EXERCISE 3.7

Write a FORMAT statement to control the reading of three floating-point numbers on a card, according to the following specifications:

> First number: 10 characters, 5 decimal places
> Second number: 8 characters, 3 decimal places
> Third number: 12 characters, no decimal places

3.89 Recent frames have illustrated FORMAT statements which contain more than one number-conversion code, indicating more than one number is to be read from a card.

The statement FORMAT (F12.4, F10.5, F6.2) denotes a total of _____ numbers per card.

three

3.90 You can also make use of an integer *before* the letter F in the FORMAT which will indicate that that number-conversion code is to be repeated that number of times in the card layout. For example, the statement FORMAT (3F12.4) is exactly equivalent to FORMAT (F12.4, F12.4, F12.4).

The statement FORMAT (3F12.4, 3F12.6) specifies a total of _____ numbers per card.

six

3.91 This count integer placed before the number-conversion code makes the writing of some FORMAT statements considerably easier. If you wished to read twelve numbers per card, six columns per number with two decimal places, the statement FORMAT (12F6.2) is obviously easier to write than to write twelve separate codes.

The statement FORMAT (12F6.2) specifies a *total* of _____ card columns.

72

3.92 A complete input or output operation, then, is defined by an input or output statement with its list of variables indicating the items involved, working together with a FORMAT which specifies the way in which these items are laid out in the cards or card images.

[true or false] The statements

> READ 1,A,X,H
> 1   FORMAT (3F12.6)

will read *one* card, reading *three* values from successive *twelve*-column fields, and place these values in A, X, and H. _____

true

3.93   The important points to remember are that the input statement list determines how much data is read while the FORMAT statement specifies how many values are contained in a particular card or card image. The combination of these items of information determines how many cards or card images are to be read.

The statement READ INPUT TAPE 2,1,(ARRAY(I), I = 1, 100) indicates that a total of _____ numbers are to be read.

100

3.94   Notice that in the last question a total of 100 values was to be read from tape 2. This many numbers obviously could not be placed on a single card image. The FORMAT statement used with this input statement, however, will only specify the contents of a *single* card image and that specification will be repeated for as many cards as are required to read in the indicated 100 values.

If FORMAT (5F12.6) were used with the input statement reading 100 values, a total of _____ card images would be required.

20

3.95   If the list of variables in an input statement is so long that it requires more than one card or card image to contain those values, the FORMAT specifications keep repeating for each new card that is read. The computer will keep on reading additional cards or card images until enough values have been read to satisfy the list.

The sequence

$$\text{READ 1,(A(I), I = 1, 1000)}$$
$$1 \quad \text{FORMAT (10F7.3)}$$

will read a total of _____ cards.

100

3.96   The relationship of input and FORMAT statements should be getting clearer now. It is very important that their respective functions be understood; otherwise, you may accidentally tell the computer to do something entirely different from that which you intend.

EXERCISE 3.8

Suppose you have written the statement READ 1,A,B,C,D,E. Construct a suitable FORMAT to specify the card location of five floating-point numbers, 14 card-columns per number with 3 decimal places each, to fit on a single card.

3.97 If a FORMAT statement specifies less than a full card's contents, the unused columns are not read by the computer. For example, the statement 1 FORMAT (5F14.5) defines the contents of 70 columns of a card; if anything were punched on the rest of the card, it would be ignored.

Using FORMAT (12F5.2) any card columns *beyond* column number _____ will be ignored.

60

3.98 If an input statement list contains less quantities than the FORMAT contains number-conversion codes, the reading process still stops when the list is satisfied. For example, the combination

READ 1,X,Y,Z
1   FORMAT (6F12.4)

will read only three quantities from the card, even though six are specified.

Using the FORMAT shown above, the statement READ 1,A,B will read *through* column _____ on the card.

24

3.99 Sometimes the number of quantities in an input statement list is not an even multiple of the number of values per card in the associated FORMAT. For example,

READ 1,(A(I), I = 1, 10)
1   FORMAT (6F12.4).

In this case, six numbers are read from the first card and four from the second; reading stops when the list is satisfied, as usual.

[true or false] Any numbers punched in columns 49 to 72 of the second card in the above example are ignored. _____

---

true

3.100 Write a READ and FORMAT combination that will read a set of monetary values into the DOLLAR array. The program has already defined N as the number of values to be read. The largest dollar value is *less* than $1,000, and you wish to pack as many numbers per card, evenly spaced, as you can (you will be including two decimal places *and* a decimal point, using 72 columns of a card).

READ _____
1   FORMAT _____

READ 1, (DOLLAR(I), I = 1,N)
1   FORMAT (12F6.2)

If your answer agrees with the one shown (except, perhaps, for choice of index variable, which is arbitrary) you may skip to Exercise 3.9 on page 110. Otherwise, continue with the next frame.

3.101   The READ statement should have been no problem unless you're getting a little rusty: N values to be read into the DOLLAR array suggest a self-indexed list, such as (DOLLAR(I),I = 1,N). Every comma and parenthesis shown here is required for *all* self-indexed lists.

The same indexed list, using J as the index variable, would be _____ .

(DOLLAR(J),J = 1,N)
The J must appear as the index *and* the dummy subscript.

3.102   The values themselves may occupy as many as six columns each: three whole-number digits (dollars), a decimal point, and two decimal places (cents). To pack these values *most* efficiently on cards, the statement FORMAT (12F6.2) is the required one for 72-column cards.

If you were permitted to use all eighty columns of a standard card, the most efficient FORMAT statement would be 1   FORMAT (_____) for this problem.

FORMAT (13F6.2)
This still wastes two columns, but this could not be helped.

3.103   Try another question about this same problem: given the statement combination

READ 1,(DOLLAR(I),I = 1,N)
1   FORMAT (12F6.2)

and a value of 40 for N, the computer would read a total of _____ cards, including any incompletely filled card.

four
If you could answer this question correctly, you are getting the knack of these input statement problems. If you are still having trouble, return to frame 3.92 for some review; otherwise, continue with Exercise 3.9.

EXERCISE 3.9

Suppose that the following ten numbers are to be read into the X array in positions 11 to 20:

11	4.5392	16	10.0835
12	12.6120	17	0.8917
13	0.7090	18	0.0001
14	7.0000	19	99.9999
15	18.4031	20	6.8329

Write a READ and FORMAT statement combination that will read all ten numbers on a single card. For this example, include a position for the decimal point in the column count of the FORMAT.

3.104 This chapter has thus far concerned itself only with floating-point number conversion in FORMAT statements. The next few frames will discuss the number-conversion codes for fixed-point data. To read numbers in the fixed-point mode, the letter I is used in the FORMAT statement. The use of this letter corresponds to the F in floating-point conversion codes, serving only to denote the mode of the numbers being read.

The statement FORMAT (I6) denotes conversion in the _____-point mode.

fixed

3.105 The letter I in a fixed-point number-conversion code is followed by an integer, just as in floating-point codes, which indicates the field width on the card or card image for the number being read. This is all the information required for fixed-point numbers, since there is no decimal fraction part.

The statement FORMAT (I20) indicates the conversion of a fixed-point number contained in columns 1 through _____ on the card.

20

3.106 Fixed-point numbers are relatively uncomplicated; that is, they are simply integer quantities and are punched on cards without decimal points. The only information needed by the computer to read a fixed-point number is the card columns in which the number is contained.

To read a five digit integer from a card, the statement FORMAT (_____) would be used.

I5

3.107 Since the variable list in an input statement may have quantities of either mode, it follows that a FORMAT statement will permit number-conversion codes of either mode in the same statement. For example, the statement FORMAT (I5,F15.4) will read two numbers, the first in fixed-point mode, the second in floating-point.

The statement FORMAT (I5, F15.4) specifies the two conversions from the first _____ columns of the card or card image.

3.108   To illustrate the mixture of modes in input statements, consider the sequence READ 1,N,X and 1   FORMAT (I20, F20.6) which will convert the number punched in columns 1 to 20 into a fixed-point integer, placing the value in N, and the number punched in 21 to 40 into a floating-point number for X.

[true or false] The use of FORMAT statement 1 above by the statement READ 1,N,M would be proper. _____

3.109   This last question raises an important point. The actual mode of conversion of the number from the card form to the computer form is specified by the FORMAT statement, with no regard to the mode of the variable which will have that value when reading is complete. This means that an error can result if you are careless.

The execution of

READ 1,N
1   FORMAT (F8.4)

will cause a _____-point number to be assigned to the variable N.

3.110   Unfortunately this doesn't work like the arithmetic formula statement N = X which would convert the mode appropriately before assigning a value to the variable. If a READ statement list variable is of the wrong mode for the conversion code in the associated FORMAT, a number actually in the wrong mode is assigned.

The sequence

READ 1,A,B
1   FORMAT (I5, F12.4)

would result in the incorrect conversion of the variable _____ .

3.111 Since the floating-point and fixed-point numbers are so drastically different inside the computer, the use of the statement sequence of the previous example would result in utter havoc when the variable A was used later in the program. There is literally no telling what would happen, and at best, the results would be meaningless.

[true or false] To prevent reading variables in the wrong mode, the variable list and the FORMAT statement should correspond in the mode used for each conversion. _____

true!
  This is a common error; you should check this part of your programs for hard-to-find bugs.

3.112 You now possess the ability to write statement combinations to read groups of numbers of either mode from either cards or card images on tape. The following items should be understood completely before continuing: *list construction* (in general, the items to be read); *self-indexed lists* (the form that permits reading several values through index definition); *F and I conversion codes* (the coded information describing the external form of the numbers); and the *list-FORMAT relationship* (that determines how many cards, etc., are read).

EXERCISE 3.10

Write a pair of statements to read 100 card images from tape 20, where each card contains two integers and three floating-point numbers to be placed in the JOE, JIM, ANDY, BOB, and FRANK arrays, respectively. Each integer occupies five card columns and each floating-point number occupies 10 columns including three decimal places. The numbers being read should be placed in the arrays in the order in which they are read.

3.113 Before going on to more details of the FORMAT statements and the output statements it would be appropriate to show you how the input data are punched on cards or arranged in card images on tape. The following frame shows a picture of a typical card which might be read with the FORMAT (3I5, 2F20.6).

3.114

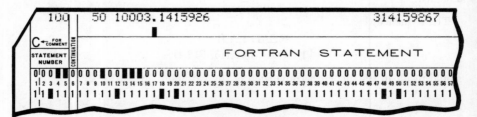

3.115   When used with a statement combination such as READ 1,I,J,K,A,B and 1   FORMAT (3I5, 2F20.6), this card, when read, would result in the following values for the variables: I would have the value 100; J, the value 50; K, the value 1000; A, the value 3.1415926; and B, the value 314.159267.

The value read for B in the example has its decimal point positioned _____ places from the right by the FORMAT statement conversion code.

3.116   Notice that all the fixed-point quantities are punched in the *rightmost* portion of their allotted fields. This must always be done with fixed-point conversion, since blank (unpunched) columns are treated as *zero* and would multiply any fixed-point value by *ten* for every blank on the right.

If a card containing *only* the number 1 punched in column 1 were read by the sequence READ 1,I,J,K,A,B and 1   FORMAT (3I5, 2F20.6), the value of the variable I would become _____ .

3.117   FORMAT (3I5, 2F20.6):

1–5	6–10	11–15	16–35	36–55	56–72	
100	50	1000	3.1415926	314159267	Not used	

Floating-point numbers *with decimal points* may be punched anywhere in their allotted fields, since the "zeroes" on the right would not affect their value. The second floating-point number read in the example given did not have a punched decimal point and this type of number must be right-adjusted the same as fixed-point numbers, since the "zeroes" on the right *are* significant.

If a card read according to FORMAT (F5.2) contained the digits 12345 in the first five columns, the value assigned to the corresponding variable would be _____ .

3.118 Because of the possibility of mispunching the data on the cards, it is strongly advised that you arrange to punch the decimal point in all floating-point numbers read from cards. This leaves no doubt as to the placement of the point, and furthermore, allows you to punch the number left-adjusted on the card, which is easier.

Using FORMAT (F5.2), a card containing .1234 punched in the first five columns would cause the corresponding variable to have the value _____ after reading.

.1234
   As punched, the presence of the decimal point overrides the FORMAT specification.

3.119 Although the preceding examples do not show this, any of the numbers punched on cards for reading by the computer may have plus or minus signs preceding the punched digits. If no sign is punched, it is assumed to be positive. Make sure that the field width specified by the FORMAT is large enough to include the sign, if used.

EXERCISE 3.11

Assuming the FORMAT (6F12.4) is to be used, show on an imaginary card layout the position of the following six numbers. Use the "natural" or right-shifted position with the decimal point punched.

(1)	1.3841	(4)	1.2345
(2)	128.3841	(5)	0.0001
(3)	1000000.0000	(6)	9.9999

3.120 The basic FORMAT statement as described in the last several frames defines the layout of a single card; when the list in the statement using the FORMAT requires more than one card's contents the same layout is repeated card after card until the list is satisfied. As shown in the next few frames, FORMAT statements may specify more than a single card layout in a single statement.

3.121 The character "/" (slash) is used in FORMAT statements to separate groups of conversion codes. These groups then specify separate card or card image layouts. For example, the statement

FORMAT (6F12.4/12F6.4)

defines two different card layouts, (6F12.4) and (12F6.4).

The statement FORMAT (15/6F12.4/12F6.4) contains a total of _____ different card layouts.

three

114

3.122 The statement FORMAT (6F12.4/12F6.4) merely tells the computer that the first card read with this FORMAT will have six numbers, floating-point, twelve columns each, etc., and the second card read will contain twelve numbers, also floating-point, six column fields, etc.

The FORMAT statement shown above specifies conversion codes for a total of _____ numbers.

18

3.123 A statement such as FORMAT (6F12.4/12F6.4) is used in cases where the cards being read are not laid out in the same manner on successive cards. If the list of an input statement using this FORMAT contained more than 18 variables, the specifications would repeat at the *beginning* of this FORMAT (first card layout).

The third card read (if any) with the FORMAT shown above would have to contain a total of _____ numbers.

six (In accordance with the first card layout)

3.124 Remember, *all* the basic FORMAT statements of recent examples would repeat their specifications with each new card that was read when the input list was long enough to require more than one card. The same condition exists in FORMAT statements defining more than one card layout.

[true or false] If 100 cards were read using FORMAT (6F12.4/12F6.4), 50 of the cards would have to contain six numbers each and the other 50 would have to contain twelve numbers each. _____

true

3.125 Consider an example.

$$READ\ 1,\ (A(I),\ I = 1,1800)$$
$$1\ \ \ FORMAT\ (6F12.4/12F6.4)$$

would cause the reading of 200 cards. The first card having six numbers, the second, twelve, the third, six, the fourth, twelve, the fifth, six, etc. The FORMAT would always repeat its specifications at the beginning of the statement, giving the alternation of card layouts.

The contents of the third card read in the above example would become the values of positions (number) _____ through _____ of the A array.

19,24

3.126 If you correctly answered the previous questions, you are getting the knack of list-FORMAT interaction very well. As long as the list keeps calling for more input, the FORMAT keeps specifying the layouts of the cards or card images repeating itself as many times as necessary.

The sequence

READ 1,X

1   FORMAT (6F12.4/12F6.4)

would cause the computer to read a total of _____ cards. (Careful now!)

3.127   A particularly desirable use of the symbol / in FORMAT statements provides for the reading of a single card according to the first card layout in the FORMAT, and then reading several cards according to the second card layout, without repeating the FORMAT specifications back at the beginning. The explanation follows.

3.128   The statement FORMAT (I6/(6F12.5)) would cause the computer to read a card, converting a single number in the fixed-point mode, then read a second card converting six floating-point numbers; assuming that the list is long enough, a third card would be read, *still* reading six floating-point numbers. The first card layout in this FORMAT is only used on the first card read! Why? Read on.

3.129   Notice anything unusual about the statement FORMAT (I6/(6F12.5))? There is an extra pair of parentheses surrounding the second card-layout specification. These parentheses cause the FORMAT specifications to repeat only the second card-layout if the input list requires more than two cards to be read.

A total of _____ number(s) would be read from the first card using the FORMAT shown above.

3.130   The general rule about repeating FORMAT specifications for long input lists is: when the end of the FORMAT statement is encountered, having used all its specifications once through, and the input list is not yet satisfied, the reading will continue, repeating the specifications at the last open parenthesis in the FORMAT statement *and continuing to the end of the FORMAT*.

The statement FORMAT (I5/I6/(12F6.4)) would require a total of_____ numbers on the fourth card read with this FORMAT.

3.131   An example of this useful feature might be

$$\text{READ 1,N,(A(I), I = 1,N)}$$
$$1 \quad \text{FORMAT (I5/(6F12.4))}$$

in which the integer read from the first card becomes the index limit for the self-indexed list. Thus the first card read determines how many successive cards will be read, using the repeating (6F12.4) specification.

If the value read above for N on the first card were 600, a *total* (be alert) of _____ cards would be read.

3.132   This last example demonstrates the most useful of the "fancy" features of FORMAT statements. You will probably find that the use of the "/" seldom occurs in input problems except for the variable length array as in that example.

[yes or no] Is anything wrong with the combination

$$\text{READ 1,N,(A(I), I = 1,N)}$$
$$1 \quad \text{FORMAT (I5, 5F12.4)?}$$

3.133   The use of parentheses in the fashion just described is limited to one level; that is, parentheses within parentheses is not permitted in FORMAT statements. When used properly, as in FORMAT (I5/(6F12.4)), a single card with a unique layout is read, followed by the reading of several cards with the second layout.

[true or false] Columns 6 to 72 of the first card would be ignored if read with the FORMAT shown above. _____

3.134   Parentheses may be used in another way in FORMAT statements where a particular sequence of conversion codes is to be repeated in the same card layout, as in FORMAT (2(I12, 2F12.4)). The conversion sequence (I12, 2F12.4), comprising 36 columns, will be repeated according to the integer preceding the parentheses.

[true or false] The FORMAT shown above appears to be the same as FORMAT (I12, 2F12.4, I12, 2F12.4). _____

3.135 Any group of conversion codes which has a repeating pattern may be enclosed in parentheses preceded by an integer, indicating the number of times that pattern is to be repeated. The total number of card columns so allotted must not exceed the size permitted for a single card, however.

The statement

$$\text{FORMAT (I12, F12.4, I12, F12.4, I12, F12.4)}$$

could be rewritten with parentheses as FORMAT (_____).

3(I12, F12.4)

3.136 The last several frames have gone through an awful lot of details about FORMAT statements. It would be wise at this point to tally the score while you catch your breath. If you are not interested in the review of the next seven frames, you may skip ahead to Exercise 3.12 on page 120.

3.137 Basically, FORMAT statements supply the computer with information about the expected layout of data on cards or card images being read, whether you use READ or READ INPUT TAPE statements. To read a list of *any* length, six numbers per card, twelve columns per number, with four decimal places, FORMAT (6F12.4) may be used.

Write a statement to specify reading of twelve fixed-point numbers per card, six columns each. _____

1 FORMAT (12I6)

3.138 If a statement such as READ INPUT TAPE 2, 1,(K(J), J = 1, 36) were used with the above FORMAT, a total of *three* card images would be read from tape unit 2, each one with the layout (12I6). The FORMAT specifications will repeat where the list in the input statement requires more than a single card's contents.

If the statement READ 1,(NUM(M), M = 1,40) were used with the above FORMAT, a total of _____ cards would be read.

four
    The fourth card would not be completely read.

3.139 Using the / to separate conversion code groups, a single FORMAT statement can specify more than one card layout for successive cards. If no interior parentheses are present in such a FORMAT, the specifications will repeat completely from the beginning if the input list is long enough.

The combination

$$\text{READ 1,(A(K), K} = 1,100)$$
$$1 \quad \text{FORMAT (6F12.2/6F12.4)}$$

will result in a total of _____ cards being read with the conversion code 6F12.4.

3.140 A multiple-card FORMAT statement such as the one described in the preceding frame can have a set of interior parentheses which enclose a complete card layout. When the input list is long enough to require the FORMAT to repeat, the repetition begins at the last open parenthesis in the FORMAT.

If 1001 numbers were read with the statement FORMAT (I5/(6F12.4)) a total of _____ of them would be converted according to the specification (6F12.4).

3.141 Yet another use of parentheses within FORMAT statements is to set off groups of conversion codes which make up repeating patterns within a single card layout. For example, FORMAT (3(I5, F10.5)) is the same effective FORMAT statement as FORMAT (I5, F10.5, I5, F10.5, I5, F10.5).

Write out the equivalent FORMAT (without interior parentheses) for the statement FORMAT (4(I5, I12)). _____

3.142 Write a suitable READ and FORMAT combination to enable the computer to:

1. Read a fixed-point integer (ten column field) and five floating-point numbers on a card, then
2. Read a group of cards, each containing six floating-point numbers
   a. *all* of the floating-point numbers are to be twelve columns in length with four decimal places
   b. the *total* number of floating-point numbers is determined by the first integer read

Choose appropriate names for the fixed-point variable, the array name, and the FORMAT number.

$$\text{READ} \underline{\hspace{4cm}}$$
$$1 \quad \text{FORMAT} \underline{\hspace{4cm}}$$

READ 1, N, (A(I), I = 1, N)
1   FORMAT (I10, 5F12.4/(6F12.4))

Your answer, short of having different variable names, should be pretty close to this one. If you note any discrepancies, check the problem statement and the suggested solution above and make sure you understand all the principles applied here.

EXERCISE 3.12

Write a READ statement to read 1000 numbers from cards into the first 1000 locations of the X array. The FORMAT should specify 8 numbers per card, 9 columns per number with 3 decimal places. Write a statement using the same FORMAT to read 1500 numbers from tape 9 into the next 1500 positions of the same X array. Show all three statements required.

3.143   You have learned how to make the computer read from cards or tape, but another very important part of a program is the part which gets the computer to disgorge its high priced answers: the output statements. The next several frames will cover this group of statements.

3.144   The most common forms of computer output are the printed page, punched cards, and magnetic tape (which contains printed page images for separate tape-to-printer operation). Large systems, like the 7090 computer, work most efficiently with magnetic tape output, since the cost of the slower card and printer operations is often prohibitive. The FORTRAN language contains statement types for all the above mentioned outputs.

3.145   To have the computer write on an attached printing device (1620, 705, 7070/7074, 704/709/790 computers) the PRINT statement is used. This consists of the word PRINT followed by a FORMAT statement number, and a list of variables subject to the same set of rules as input lists.

The statement PRINT 1,A,B,C refers to FORMAT statement _____ .

1

3.146   The PRINT statement operates as follows: the values of the variables in the list are output in the order listed and printed on the attached printing device, according to the indicated FORMAT statement. Like the input statements, the list of variables serves only to supply the computer with the quantities involved.

The statement PRINT 1, (A(I), I = 1, 100) will print a total of _____ values of the A array.

3.147   The variable list in the PRINT statement (or any other output statement) performs the usual function: it defines the variables whose values are to be printed. The list may contain variables of either mode and may make use of the self-indexed form; the variables may have subscripts as long as they are not mathematical expressions other than the accepted forms (see 1.155).

The statement PRINT 100,A,B,C,I,J,K will cause the computer to print a total of _____ values.

3.148   The FORMAT statement is used in PRINT statements in much the same way as in input statements; it defines the layout of the numbers in the external medium (the printed line or line image or the punched card layout) and it uses the same conversion codes as the input FORMAT statements.

[true or false] The FORMAT statements used with PRINT statements can use I and F conversions. _____

3.149   The operation of a PRINT and FORMAT combination is best described by an example. PRINT 1,A,B,C and 1   FORMAT (F20.4) will direct the computer to print three lines, each line containing a single number within a space of 20 print columns with 4 decimal places to the right of the decimal point.

If statement 1 in the above example had been 1   FORMAT (2F20.4) the computer would print a total of _____ lines.

3.150   The FORMAT statement used with an output statement will define the layout of a single line. The writing process continues until the list is satisfied, repeating line after line in the same layout, similar to the card reading process covered earlier.

The combination

$$\text{PRINT } 1, (A(K), K = 1, 100)$$
$$1 \quad \text{FORMAT } (10F12.4)$$

will print a total of _____ lines.

3.151 The printed line on the 7090 computer's attached printer contains 120 characters, as does the separate printer which performs the tape-to-printer operation (the card and card image length was 72 columns, remember). This means that FORMAT statements for PRINT statements can specify a total of 120 columns of field width.

[true or false] The statement 1 FORMAT (20F20.5) is a legal FORMAT for printing. _____

3.152 Incidentally, the decimal point is printed for floating-point numbers, and its position is rigidly dictated by the second integer after the F in the conversion code. The input condition, you will remember, permitted the decimal point to be anywhere as long as it was punched, or the FORMAT information was used if not punched.

The statement FORMAT (12F10.5) will print a line of twelve numbers, each of which has _____ decimal places to the right of the decimal point.

five

3.153 Remember, the computer does not know what digits are significant with respect to the computation being done. It is up to the programmer to analyze the printed information for accuracy as to the number of decimal places being printed; the computer will print exactly what you call for, even if some of the digits are not significant.

[true or false] If you are computing with two-place accuracy, you would not use a statement like FORMAT (F20.5). _____

3.154 Another point: the printed numbers always appear right-adjusted in their allotted fields. This means that you can space the numbers on the printed page by making the assigned field width accordingly wider than is needed to contain the printed number. The excess space in the field will be left blank, providing spacing.

If you use FORMAT (F20.6) to print the value 23.456789 (including the point) you will have a total of _____ blanks to the left of the printed number.

eleven

3.155 The use of PRINT statements is actually that simple; once you have mastered input statements, many of the same features and conventions carry over into the output statement family. To illustrate, a statement combination such as PRINT 1, (A(I), I = 1, 1000) and 1 FORMAT (10F12.4) will print out 100 lines of print, each line containing 10 values from the A array.

The first printed line in the example above will contain values from positions _____ to _____ of the A array.

3.156 The output FORMAT statements may include conversion codes of either or both modes in a single FORMAT. As was the case with input data, the FORMAT code determines the mode of conversion, and if the variable whose value is being printed is of the wrong mode, the printed result is meaningless (often a rather wild number).

The combination

$$\text{PRINT 1, A}$$
$$1 \quad \text{FORMAT (15)}$$

will result in the value of A being printed in the _____-point mode.

3.157 The problem of matching the modes of the quantities being read or written and the modes of the corresponding conversion codes is brought up again to emphasize its importance. Many error conditions can be caught and diagnosed by the computer, but this is not one of them. Programs with these bugs often behave strangely.

[true or false] The combination

$$\text{PRINT 1,A,B,C,I,J}$$
$$1 \quad \text{FORMAT (3F20.6,2I10)}$$

is perfectly valid with respect to the correspondence of the modes. _____

3.158 You can easily check your programs to ensure that this error condition does not exist. Any input or output list has a definite order in which the variables' values are to be input or output, and every FORMAT statement has a definite cyclic order of conversion codes, even if repetition is called for. Taking a dry run and reading the program as the computer would will often show up situations where such errors exist.

[true or false] The combination PRINT 1, N, (A(I), I = 1, 100), 1   FORMAT (15,5F20.6) will result in incorrect conversion of some of the data. _____

true

3.159 The use of the PRINT statement, then, is very similar to the use of any of the input statements. The general form of construction is the same: identifying word PRINT, a FORMAT number, and a suitable list of variables whose values are to be printed. The FORMAT statement performs the same function for the PRINT statement as it does for input statements: specifying the layout of the data in the external medium.

3.160 Sample program segment.

(The following frame contains a schematic showing the placement of the values on the printed page resulting from these statements, using the name to show position.)

$$\text{PRINT 15, (X(I), I = 1, 80)}$$
$$\text{15   FORMAT (8F10.4)}$$

X[(1)]	X[(2)]	X[(3)]	X[(4)]	X[(5)]	X[(6)]	X[(7)]	X[(8)]
X[(9)]	X[(10)]	X[(11)]	X[(12)]	X[(13)]	X[(14)]	X[(15)]	X[(16)]
X[(17)]	X[(18)]	X[(19)]	X[(20)]	X[(21)]	X[(22)]	X[(23)]	X[(24)]

. . . .

X[(73)]   X[(74)]   X[(75)]   X[(76)]   X[(77)]   X[(78)]   X[(79)]   X[(80)]

Write a combination of statements which will write on the attached printer, using a full 120-column line, the entire contents of the 600 word BLOCK array, six numbers per line, and two decimal places for each number.

_____
_____

PRINT 1, (BLOCK(I), I = 1, 600)
1   FORMAT (6F20.2)

If your answer agrees with this one (excepting, of course, the choice of index name and FORMAT number) you may skip to Exercise 3.13 on page 125. If you did not obtain the correct result, continue with the next frame.

3.161 First of all, we will examine the PRINT statement (if you had no trouble with this, go on to the next frame now). After the word PRINT, you place your selected FORMAT statement number and follow this with the list (it was assumed that you would use self-indexed form rather than write out a list of 600 variable names with subscripts). The self-indexed form consists of the name (BLOCK), its dummy subscript, and the index definition (1 to 600).

Write a suitable PRINT statement to write out a 20-word array called MATRIX (use FORMAT 1). _____

PRINT 1,(MATRIX(I), I = 1, 20)

3.162 As for the FORMAT, you were asked to specify a *full* line (120 columns) containing *six* numbers (obviously there must be *20* columns per number provided) with two decimal places. The mode is plainly floating-point for the variable BLOCK. The only possible statement to fit these conditions is 1   FORMAT (6F20.2).

Write a suitable statement to specify the layout of a printed line containing *ten* numbers of *twelve* columns each, all floating-point, with *six* decimal places.

FORMAT (10F12.6)

3.163 Try another similar problem. Write a set of statements to control the writing of the array called VECTOR which contains 1000 values. These are to be printed, twenty per line on a full line, with one decimal place. _____

PRINT 1,(VECTOR(I), I = 1, 1000)
1   FORMAT (20F6.1)

If your answer agrees with the one shown, you are getting the hang of this output business. If not, better go back to frame 3.144 and review before continuing.

EXERCISE 3.13

Given three 100 number arrays—A, B, and C—write a PRINT and FORMAT combination to list these arrays in three parallel columns of numbers. Each column of numbers should occupy 20 character columns of the printer with four decimal places provided. This should result in 100 lines being printed, each line having 3 numbers.

3.164 So far, the discussion of output statements has concerned itself only with printing on attached printing devices. Another means of output is the use of magnetic tapes, where an actual printer image is stored on the tape for future printing.

3.165 You will remember that cards and card images were read by similar statements, differing only in their identifying words. The same is true for tape-writing statements; they are made up exactly like PRINT statements, using the words WRITE OUTPUT TAPE i, (where i is a tape unit number; note the comma). The words and tape number are followed by a FORMAT number, of course, and an output list.

The statement WRITE OUTPUT TAPE 3,1,A,B,C causes the computer to write on tape _____ .

3.166 The only difference between the WRITE OUTPUT TAPE and PRINT statements is, literally, their identifying wording. Whatever you write on the attached printer, you may also write on tape for separate tape-to-printer operation in exactly the same formats.

Change the statement PRINT 1, (A(I), I = 1, 100) such that the same information will be written on tape unit 8. _____

3.167 The tape unit numbers used both for WRITE OUTPUT TAPE and READ INPUT TAPE statements will vary for different types of computers. A quick check of any computing center will reveal the available tape unit numbers.

Write a pair of statements to write the contents of the BLOCK array on tape 12 so that each line image will contain 10 numbers, 12 columns per number, with 5 decimal places. The BLOCK array has a total of 1000 numbers.

_____

_____

3.168 The writing statement should present no real problem; all you need is the words WRITE OUTPUT TAPE followed by the tape number (12), a FORMAT number (e.g., 1) and the self-indexed list for the BLOCK array (BLOCK(I), I = 1, 1000). With appropriately placed commas, the correct statement becomes:

WRITE OUTPUT TAPE 12, 1, (BLOCK(I), I = 1, 1000)

Write a tape-writing statement to output the contents of a 500-number array called GROUP; use tape 3. _____

3.169 The FORMAT required in the original problem was to specify a ten-number line with twelve columns per number and five decimal places. The only combination to achieve this is 1   FORMAT (10F12.5).

Write a FORMAT statement to specify eight numbers of fifteen columns each, four decimal places. 1   FORMAT (_____)

3.170   Write a pair of statements to write the 100-number A array on tape 6 so that, when printed, the numbers will evenly fill ten lines (two decimal places for each number).

_____

_____

EXERCISE 3.14

Tape unit 11 contains 100 card images, each of which consists of 10 floating-point numbers, 7 characters per number with 3 decimal places. Write a program to copy these 100 card images onto tape 12 exactly as they appear on tape 11 (hint: same FORMAT). Use a 10-number array as a buffer; that is, read ten numbers into the array and then write them onto the second tape before reading the next 10 numbers.

3.171   This chapter has, so far, introduced five new statement types:

READ	READ INPUT TAPE
PRINT	WRITE OUTPUT TAPE
FORMAT	

3.172   There are other input and output statements in the FORTRAN language, all of which have similar characteristics to those covered so far. They may be found in the appropriate manuals and their use can be learned easily on the student's own part; consequently, they will not be covered in this manual.

Instead, the remainder of this chapter will be devoted to additional features of the output statements already covered.

3.173 FORMAT statements are constructed identically for input or output statement use, with the exception that output FORMAT statements may have longer total field specifications for tape and printer than are allowed for cards. By the same token, many of the features demonstrated for input FORMATS are useful for output statement use also.

3.174 The use of the / in an output FORMAT has the same basic meaning as it did for the input FORMAT; it will signify the end of one line or line image specification and the beginning of the next. Thus, the same statement can specify consecutive lines with different specifications.

The statement FORMAT (5F20.5/6F20.6) will specify a total of _____ numbers on the first line, a total of _____ on the second, and, if the list contains enough quantities, a third line would contain _____ .

5, 6, 5

3.175 The use of interior parentheses to establish a repetition point is useful for output FORMAT statements too. The example FORMAT (3I10/(6F20.6)) would cause the printing of a line of fixed-point quantities followed by several lines of floating-point numbers (assuming the list is long enough).

The statement PRINT 1,I,J,K,(A(I), I = 1, 60) used with the FORMAT shown above would result in a total of _____ lines of fixed-point numbers and _____ lines of floating-point numbers.

one, ten

3.176 One interesting effect concerns the use of more than one "/" in an output FORMAT; every adjacent pair of slashes will cause a blank line to be printed (that is, // will cause one blank line, /// will cause two, etc.). Thus the FORMAT (3I10///(6F20.4)) would specify printing a line of numbers, *two* blanks, and more lines of numbers. This feature can be used to good advantage for spacing lines of numbers on printed pages.

The statement FORMAT (6F20.5////(5F24.6)) will provide for _____ blank lines after the first.

three

3.177 Another interesting feature, available on output statements only, is the ability to print the index value of a self-indexed list without actually generating a separate variable. For example, the statement PRINT 1, (I,A(I), I = 1, 10), which lists the index variable I separately, will print out values in the following order: the value 1, the value of A(1), the number 2, the value of A(2), etc.

A total of _____ values will be printed by the statement shown above.

3.178 Input and output with FORTRAN is actually very straightforward and fairly consistent, even though there are many details to remember. Experience with this language and others makes one appreciate the ease of using FORTRAN input/output, however.

Warning! In output situations, beware of assigning a field width that is too small to contain the number being printed. You may *lose* part of those precious answers. The condition is similar to overflow in mathematical operations; the excess digits are lopped off at the *high* end (the most significant digits!).

If you tried to write out the value 5280.00 with FORMAT (F6.2) the number printed (including the decimal point) would be _____ .

3.179 One last, but very important, feature of output statements is the ability to write alphabetic characters on the printer. This is useful for labeling the answers, titling the output listing pages, etc. The writing of alphabetic information is accomplished with a new conversion code: the H conversion.

[true or false] The computer can write English text through the use of the H conversion code. _____

3.180 Alphabetic information that is to be printed (or written on tape for later printing) is written verbatim into the FORMAT statement. It is always immediately preceded by the letter H, which is preceded in turn by an integer that is a count of the number of characters following the H to be included in the printed information, including blanks.

[true or false] By the above definition FORMAT (18HTHIS IS ALPHABETIC) is a valid statement. _____

3.181 Whenever a FORMAT statement containing an H conversion code is used by an output statement, the information defined after the H code is printed (or written on tape) exactly as it was written into the FORMAT at the time the program was compiled.

[true or false] The statement FORMAT(8H FORTRAN) would print the word FORTRAN when used with a PRINT statement. _____

3.182 In other words, if you wanted to title a printed page with a 100-character sentence you would merely write 100H followed by the actual sentence, writing this directly in the FORMAT statement. This alphabetic information is then available for output any time that FORMAT is called upon by an output statement.

To provide the word OUTPUT as a page heading, you would write FORMAT (_____).

3.183 Actually the information following the H code is not restricted to alphabetic characters; you may use all 26 alphabetic characters, all ten numeric digits, and the special characters +, −, *, /, =, $, (,), period, comma, and blank. Even blank characters to space words must be counted in the integer before the H.

Fill in the statement FORMAT (_____ HOUTPUT DATA).

3.184 The count integer preceding all H codes must include the exact amount of information that is to be printed—no more, no less. If the count is either too large or too small the FORMAT will probably be invalid, and certainly the intended information would not be correctly represented. (NOTE: all future examples will denote a blank, where it must be counted, with a small letter *b*; the *b*'s, of course, would never actually be printed as part of a statement.)

Fill in the statement FORMAT (_____ H*b*THIS*b*IS*b*THE*b*OUTPUT*b* DATA).

3.185 Unlike the F and I conversion codes, the H code does not have a corresponding variable in an output list. Instead, the computer simply places the information into the output image wherever it is called for in a FORMAT.

[true or false] The sequence

PRINT 1

1   FORMAT (19H*b*JOE*b*DOE,*b*DEPT.*b*241)

would title a page with the sentence

JOE DOE, DEPT. 241

3.186   The H code can be used in the same FORMAT with either F or I codes. For example, the statement

1   FORMAT (14H*b*THE*b*ANSWER*b*IS,F15.5)

would be perfectly valid. If used, say, with the statement PRINT 1,X the computer would print first the indicated alphabetic information (14 columns) and then the value of the variable X (the next 15 columns).

If X had a value of 1.23456 in the example above, the printed line would be _____ .

*b*THE*b*ANSWER*b*IS*bbbbbbbb*1.23456 (Including blanks as *b*).

3.187   The H code, then, can be used anywhere in an output FORMAT to provide the ability to write words or symbols to clarify your output. These H conversion sequences can be preceded or followed by F or I conversion codes, but care must be taken to ensure that the count is accurate! The H field may be as long as desired, as long as it does not exceed the allowable print-line size (also, the H field plus any F or I fields must not exceed this figure).

3.188   The characters printed with H conversion codes may be alphabetic, numeric, or special characters. This type of information is given the name "alphanumeric" (or sometimes, "alphameric") to distinguish between this type and purely numeric data as converted by F and I codes. The former will be used in this manual.

Alphanumeric information is output with the _____(letter) conversion code.

H

3.189   An interesting combination of the H code and the repeating FORMAT features enables you to title a printed page and follow this with an array of numbers, using just a single FORMAT statement. The sample program on the following page will print a line of alphanumeric information, skip a line, and print an array.

3.190   Sample program segment:

PRINT 1, (A(I), I = 1, 1000)
1   FORMAT (8H*b*A*b*ARRAY//(10F12.4))

3.191   Notice that the line of alphanumeric information will be printed only once; the inner parentheses will keep the output statement's list of 1000 quantities repeating with the (10F12.4) specification. That inner parentheses set is very important in this example; without this, the *entire* FORMAT specification would be repeated, including the alphanumeric information.

[true or false] If the inner parentheses were omitted in the example of frame 3.190, the computer would print in alternating fashion: "A ARRAY", ten numbers, "A ARRAY", ten numbers, "A ARRAY", ten numbers, etc. _____

3.192   H conversion, then, is just a handy way of writing words, symbols, and labels to label your output. The rules are fairly simple; any alphanumeric information that you wish to print is written directly in a FORMAT preceded by the letter H and an integer telling how many characters in the alphanumeric field. Every time that FORMAT is called upon by an output statement (or repeated) that field is reproduced on the printer or tape.

Write a set of statements to print the following line:

*b*RESULTS*b*FROM*b*NEWTON*b*METHOD*b*

followed by a blank line (skipped line) and the contents of the 50-number ANSWER array, ten numbers per full line and six decimal places per number.

PRINT _____

1   FORMAT _____

PRINT 1, (ANSWER(I), I = 1, 50)
1   FORMAT (28H*b*RESULTS*b*FROM*b*NEWTON*b*METHOD*b*//
(10F12.6))

If your answer agrees with the one shown, skip to Exercise 3.15 on page 133. If you do not agree with this answer, continue with the next frame.

3.193   The PRINT statement was probably no trouble. The list was self-indexed for the 50-number ANSWER array. The FORMAT statement, on the other hand, could be tricky. You were asked to start the printing with a line of alphanumeric information. This means that you start the FORMAT statement with that H field:

(28H*b*RESULTS*b*FROM*b*NEWTON*b*METHOD*b*. . .

There are a total of _____ characters in the H field shown above, including blanks (but not including the letter H itself).

3.194 You were expected to skip a line after printing this title, so the consecutive slash marks "//" should follow the alphanumeric field. This will allow the computer to print the alphanumeric field, skip the following line, and then look on further in the FORMAT for the remaining specifications.

Write a FORMAT which will specify the writing of the word *b*ANSWER*b*, skip two lines, and specify a 20-column fixed-point number field. _____

FORMAT (8H*b*ANSWER*b*///I20)

3.195 The FORMAT statement requested for the problem of three frames back would be completed by the addition of the F code for the array to be printed. You were told that there would be ten numbers per full line and six decimal places, meaning, for a 120-character line, that you would use (10F12.6).

Printing a 50-number array with the specification (10F12.6) would result in a total of _____ lines.

five
    If you feel that your misunderstandings have been cleared up, you may continue with Exercise 3.15. If questions still remain unanswered, turn to frame 3.179 and review before continuing.

EXERCISE 3.15

Write a combination of statements to print the heading shown below.

bFINALbCOMPUTEDbRESULTS

Following this heading, skip a line and print a column of ten values of the ANSWER array, using 20 columns of print characters with two decimal places included. Use a *single* FORMAT statement for this problem.

3.196 An additional conversion code for FORMAT statements which proves useful for spacing portions of your output on a given line is the X conversion, consisting of an integer followed by the letter X. This code merely causes a certain number of blank columns to be inserted in the output image, the number of blanks being defined by the integer preceding the letter X.

The statement FORMAT (F14.4,10X,F12.6) will cause the placement of _____ blanks between the two F conversions.

ten

3.197 Use of the X code in the FORMAT statement would effect the same result as an H field with nothing but blank characters. For example, the statements

> FORMAT (. . . , 20X, . . .) and
> FORMAT (. . . , 20H*bbbbbbbbbbbbbbbbbbbb*, . . .)

are equivalent, but the former is obviously more compact.

Write a FORMAT statement whose output will consist of ten blanks, the *letter* A, twenty blanks, the *letter* B, twenty blanks, the *letter* C, forty blanks, and the *letters* ERROR, making use of X and H conversions.

> FORMAT (_____)

FORMAT (10X, 1HA, 20X, 1HB, 20X, 1HC, 40X, 5HERROR)

3.198 The attached printing device (and separate tape-to-printer machine) for most computer systems does *not* actually *print* the first character in the output image. This character is interpreted by the printing device as a "carriage-control" character which causes the printer to space down the page in various ways.

In the statement FORMAT (7H*b*ANSWER), the first character (carriage-control character) is _____ .

---

b (blank)

3.199 This fact holds true whether the first item in the print image is a result of a numeric field (F or I conversion) or alphanumeric field (H conversion). The best way to think of this is to picture a printed line image where the first character, whatever it is, will not be printed and the second character in the image will be the first character in the line that is actually printed (you may recall that previous examples have had blanks there).

[true or false] The very *first* character in any printed-line image is not printed.

---

true

3.200 On the 704/709/790 computer systems, the following characters, appearing in column one of a printed-line image, will cause the indicated carriage-control operation to occur.

b (blank)	Normal (single) space
0 (zero)	Double space
1 (one)	Skip to a new page

In all cases, the indicated control is executed *before* the actual line is printed.

3.201   Programming the desired carriage-control character into the print image (either for the attached printer or for a tape print-image) will give the programmer a useful control of his printed output. For example, if you wish your output to begin on a fresh page in the printer, FORMAT (1H1) used with a PRINT statement will accomplish this. Of course, the character 1 could have been part of a larger FORMAT, too.

The carriage-control character in FORMAT (10X, 6HANSWER) would be
_____ .

3.202   If you answered this correctly, you have probably grasped the meaning of this concept pretty well. The statement FORMAT (10X, 6HANSWER) sets up a printed-line image of ten blanks and the word ANSWER. Therefore, nine blanks and the word ANSWER will be printed, with the first blank acting as carriage-control. Remember, it is the first character in the *image* which has this function, not the first character in the FORMAT statement itself!

3.203   While the carriage-control feature can be very helpful, it also can do strange things if you do not handle it carefully. There are many ways in which an odd character can unintentionally appear in the first column of the printed-line image. The next few frames will cite a few common examples you should watch out for.

PRINT 1,X,Y,Z

1   FORMAT (14H1THE*b*ANSWER*b*IS,F15.5)

3.204   In this case, the intent was to start printing the answers on a new page, so the character 1 was placed in the print image; unfortunately, the FORMAT must repeat to print all the quantities in the list, resulting in a complete page skip each time (on some of the faster printers, this can be spectacular).

PRINT 1, NUMBER

1   FORMAT (I2)

3.205   This looks harmless enough, but what if the value of number were 10? The print image would consist of the characters 1 and 0, the first of which, of course, will be the carriage-control; only the zero would be printed (after a page skip). Numbers that fill their allotted field may perform accidental control like this.

PRINT 1, (A(I), I = 1, 1000)

1   FORMAT (12HTHE*b*A*b*MATRIX//(10F12.6))

3.206   Look all right? There are no repetitions of the alphanumeric field, and the numbers can be assumed to be small enough to fit well within twelve column fields. Look again at the alpha numeric field—the *first* character is the letter T which will cause a strange skip (and won't be printed!).

135

3.207   The three preceding frames have illustrated simple bugs that can easily crop up in even the most carefully written programs. To be safe, always check your FORMAT statements to see that you did not inadvertently place some odd character in the first position of the image; in multiple-line FORMAT statements check *each* line.

This concludes the material on input and output statements in the FORTRAN language. At this point you can go on to the next page and take the examination for this chapter.

PART 3: EXAMINATION

1. Indicate the number of numerical values read or written by each of the following statement groups:

   (a) READ 1, A, B, C, D: _____
   (b) PRINT 1, (Y(I), I = 1,25), Z: _____
   (c) I = 11:
       J = 20:
       READ INPUT TAPE 2,1,(X(N),N = I,J): _____
   (d) PRINT 2: _____
   (e) READ 1,(A(I), B(I), C(I), I = 1,5): _____
   (f) PRINT 10, (J, X(J), J = 1, 100): _____
   (g) WRITE OUTPUT TAPE 3,50,(X(I), I = 1, 10),(Y(J),J = 1,15,2):
       _____
   (h) I = 1
       J = 10
       K = 21
       L = 2
       PRINT 1,(BLOCK(N),N = I,K,J),(ARRAY(M),M = I,K,L): _____
   (i) READ 21, I,J,K,(A(L),L = 1,10): _____
   (j) I = 20
       J = 50
       K = 3 * I/J
       N = I * J
       PRINT 101, (X(M), M = K,N,1), Y,Z: _____

2. How many *values* per line or card will be read or written according to the following FORMAT statements:

   (a) FORMAT (6F12.4): _____
   (b) FORMAT (F10.2, 20X, 3I5): _____
   (c) FORMAT (20Hb TABULAR b OUTPUT b NO. b, I2): _____
   (d) FORMAT (6(F12.4, I8)): _____
   (e) FORMAT (F16.0, 10X, F8.2, 7I8): _____
   (f) FORMAT (F12.6, 2(3F6.2, 10X, I6)): _____
   (g) FORMAT (3HbX=, F10.4, 3X, 3HbY=, F10.4): _____
   (h) FORMAT (F12.4/(12X,F12.4)): _____
   (i) FORMAT (72(1H *)): _____
   (j) FORMAT (2(F12.6, 6X, I4), 6F6.0): _____

3. Write a complete program (with STOP and END statements provided) to do the following.

   (a) Read a card containing a fixed-point number ranging from 1 to 10,000 in card columns 1 to 5.

(b) Read that many floating-point numbers from *successive* cards, six numbers per card, twelve columns per number (including four decimal places), to make up the A array.

(c) Sort the array values into algebraically ascending order without using a separate array (use the technique of comparing adjacent values, swapping if they are out of order).

(d) Print out the reordered array, ten numbers per line, twelve columns (four decimal places) per number.

(e) Stop the computer.

4. Write a program to read 1000 card images from tape unit 2. These images contain current information about an employee stock-purchasing plan. Each image is laid out as follows:

Column	Contents	Range
1–5	Employee serial number	10000-99999
11–16	Current account balance	$0.00-$999.99
20–22	Number of shares owned	0-999

Your program should read these quantities into three individual 1000-number arrays, and then read 1000 cards, each of which contains the following updating information:

Column	Contents	Range
1–5	Employee serial number	10000-99999
11–16	Amount deposited this period	$0.00-$999.99

reading these values into two additional 1000-number arrays.

Finally, your program is to read a single card containing the current stock price, six columns with two decimal positions provided. Then, taking each employee updating (card) record in turn, find each *card* serial number's position in the *tape* list and add the corresponding new *deposit* to the corresponding *account balance*. Check this total against the current price, and subtract the current price if the employee has purchased a share, simultaneously updating his "shares owned" total and printing his serial number on the attached printer. When this has been done for all 1000 employees, write a new tape (unit 3) containing the updated version of the three 1000-number arrays, using the same FORMAT as before. (Assume that no new deposit will exceed the stock price, and also that every serial number in the updating card deck will be found somewhere in the tape list.)

PART 4

FUNCTION NOTATION,
SUBPROGRAMMING,
SPECIFICATION STATEMENTS

Parts 1, 2, and 3 have introduced you to the three basic elements of scientific programming languages—arithmetic, control, and input/output—as they are programmed in the FORTRAN language. The features presented in this part give considerable added flexibility to the FORTRAN language through *subprograms,* which are program segments executed under the control of another program. These subprograms are usually tailored to perform some often repeated set of operations; a subprogram is written only once, but may be used again and again either in a single program setup or in different programs. In either case duplication of effort is avoided by eliminating the need for rewriting program segments to perform these common operations.

Also included in this chapter are the specification statements which provide the computer with necessary information about the program (such as array sizes) but are not executed in the sense that arithmetic formula statements are.

4.1 You have become familiar with mathematical expressions as used in arithmetic formula statements and IF statements. Through the use of the arithmetic formula statement, we can tell the computer to perform all kinds of basic mathematical operations.

4.2 Through the use of the basic arithmetic operations, we can perform many more complicated functions such as trigonometric functions, logarithms, and roots. All these types of functions can be computed approximately with simple arithmetic operations of addition, subtraction, multiplication, and division.

4.3 Since many of these complicated functions can be represented by a series of mathematical operations, it follows that these operations can be programmed for a computer. With the FORTRAN system of subprograms these functions can be made available to any program which might use them.

[true or false] A function such as the trigonometric sine can be programmed for the computer. _____

true

4.4 If every computer programmer wrote a program to compute, for example, the trigonometric sine, there would be an enormous amount of duplication of effort; therefore, many FORTRAN systems provide a package of previously written programs to compute such common functions for your programs.

The programs that compute these functions are under the control of your program, and as such are called _____ .

subprograms

4.5 The package of programs provided for FORTRAN users is called a "library" and the programs contained in the library are called "library functions."

The use of these library programs is very simple and will be explained in the next few frames.

FORTRAN provides a set of subprograms in the _____.

4.6   Every function subprogram in the library has a particular *name* associated with it. If you wish to make use of a function subprogram in the library all you have to do is use its name in a FORTRAN expression in the same fashion that you would do with a variable.

A subprogram can be brought into use by mentioning its _____.

4.7   It is actually that simple. If you wished to compute the trigonometric sine for the value of X, for example, you might write the statement Y = SINF(X) which would place the sine value in Y. This statement in your program would automatically make use of the sine program in the library.

[true or false] The sine program as used in the example above is a subprogram.

_____

4.8   All library functions are programs which compute some functional relation of a single quantity called an "argument." In the example using the sine function, the argument is the angle whose sine is to be computed; that is, in the statement Y = SINF(X) the variable X is the argument.

[true or false] The statement shown above is an arithmetic formula statement.

_____

4.9   All library functions in the standard package have *one* argument. This argument is the quantity that the function uses to compute the desired result. In a sense, the argument is an input quantity to the subprogram.

In the statement Z = SINF(THETA) the argument is the variable _____.

4.10   When a function subprogram is called upon by mention of its name in an expression, the computer actually stops executing your program while it computes the function value. When the subprogram is finished executing, the computer comes back to your program with the computed result.

In the statement $Y = SINF(A)$, the value whose sine will be computed is the variable _____ .

4.11 The function name may be used in an expression exactly like a variable name. When computing the expression, the function's value for the current value of the argument replaces the function name in the expression; this is similar to the way in which a variable works, with the value replacing the name.

The statement $Y = A * SINF(X) + B * SINF(Z)$ calls upon the sine function a total of _____ times.

4.12 The foregoing example, $Y = A * SINF(X) + B * SINF(Z)$, demonstrates the flexibility of the function notation. More than one function may appear in a single expression and the same function may be used more than once in a single statement. In the above case, the value of the sine of X will be multiplied by A, the value of the sine of Z will be multiplied by B and these values will be added.

The final computed result of the expression shown above will become the value of the variable _____ .

4.13 As mentioned before, every function has a unique name. When the function is used in a statement, its name is followed by a pair of parentheses containing the argument. The examples used in the preceding frames have shown one of these functions with its argument, as in $SINF(X)$.

The argument in the expression $SQRTF(ARG)$ is the variable _____ .

4.14 The argument may be a variable, constant, or any legal expression. Thus, $SINF(X)$, $SINF(3.1415926)$, or $SINF(A ** 2 + B ** 2)$ are legal examples of arguments. In any case, when a function name appears in a statement the value of the argument is determined *first,* then the function is executed to obtain the result.

The argument in the expression $SINF(X ** 2)$ is _____ .

4.15 As a matter of fact, the argument of a function can even be another function itself. $SINF(SQRTF(X))$ is an example of nested functions. In cases like this, the innermost function (the one that is also an argument) is evaluated first to obtain a value for use of the outer function as an argument.

In the example SINF(SQRTF(X)) the function named _____ is an argument of another function.

4.16   Library functions are available for the 650, 705, 7070/7074, and 704/709/7090 versions of FORTRAN. The standard library distributed with the 704/709/7090 system contains seven functions for mathematical computation. These appear in the following frame with explanations.

4.17

Library Functions Available with 704/709/7090 FORTRAN Systems

SINF(A)	Trigonometric sine	$\sin A$	arg. in radians
COSF(A)	Trigonometric cosine	$\cos A$	arg. in radians
TANHF(A)	Hyperbolic tangent	$\tanh A$	arg. in radians
ATANF(A)	Arc-tangent	$\tan^{-1} A$	
SQRTF(A)	Square root	$\sqrt{A}$	arg. ≥ 0
EXPF(A)	Exponential	e^A	
LOGF(A)	Natural logarithm	$\log_e A$	

4.18   It is possible to add library function programs at individual computing centers, so it would be advisable to check with the computing center to find out what additional library programs, if any, are available. The standard set of programs shown in the preceding frame covers only a few of the common functions.

4.19   An obvious restriction exists: no variable should be named identically to a function in the library. Remember that the function name is used as a variable in the expression, and the accidental use of a variable name that was also a function name could cause the function to be employed.

Check the blanks below with a plus sign for legal variable names and a minus for illegal variable names:

X12345 _____   ABCDE _____   SINF _____

32K _____   IJKLMNO _____   X! $\sqrt{\pi}$ ∫ ? _____

4.20   Two main points have been covered so far: (1) a set of commonly used subprograms in function form is available to your programs in a library; (2) these function subprograms are brought into use by the mention of the appropriate name in an ordinary FORTRAN expression, using the name like a variable.

[true or false] A function name must be accompanied by the correct number of arguments. _____

true

4.21 All the library functions in the standard package are written to use floating-point arguments and all the functions yield floating-point values for their result. This means that they must be used in a floating-point expression and must have floating-point quantities for their argument.

[true or false] The expression SINF(I) is legal. _____

false
(The argument of the SINF function program must be floating-point.)

4.22 Since the function's name is a part of an ordinary FORTRAN expression, and its value is used directly in the computation indicated in the expression, it is very important that the mode agrees properly with the entire expression.

[true or false] The statement Y = I * SINF(X − Y) is legal. _____

false
The variable I is a fixed-point quantity and cannot be used with the value of SINF.

4.23 In general, then, library function names can be used in any way which is legal for ordinary variables. In fact, their meaning is very similar to that of a variable name; when the expression containing a function name is executed, the current value for that function is computed and supplied to the expression to be used as indicated (as is the value of a variable).

Write a statement to compute the product of three quantities, 2.0 times the sine of X times the cosine of X, placing the result in the variable ANSWER. Note the list of available library functions: _____

SINF(A)	SQRTF(A)
COSF(A)	EXPF(A)
TANHF(A)	LOGF(A)
ATANF(A)	

ANSWER = 2.0 * SINF(X) * COSF(X)
It is true that the expression SINF(2. * X) is equivalent by identity.
If your answer agrees with the one shown above, skip to frame 4.27; if your answer does not agree with the one indicated as correct, continue with the next frame.

4.24   The problem requires an arithmetic formula statement with two function names in the expression. The expression was to have computed the product of three terms: 2.0, sin X, and cos X. The use of the functions' names with their given arguments in an ordinary expression is sufficient to solve this problem.

[true or false] When an expression containing a function is computed, the computed value of the function replaces the function name in the expression.

_____

true

4.25   The expression given in the preceding problem required the computation of sin X and cos X. The functions in the library to compute these quantities are SINF and COSF; in this problem they both had the argument X. Therefore, the complete expression to solve for the product has to be 2.0 * SINF(X) * COSF(X).

Given that sin(0.) = 0. and that cos(0.) = 1.0, the value of the expression 2.0 * SINF(X) * COSF(X) would be _____ when X has a value of 0. Use the list of available library functions.

$$
\begin{array}{ll}
\text{SINF(A)} & \text{SQRTF(A)} \\
\text{COSF(A)} & \text{EXPF(A)} \\
\text{TANHF(A)} & \text{LOGF(A)} \\
\text{ATANF(A)} &
\end{array}
$$

0.
    2.0 times 0. times 1.

4.26   Try a similar problem requiring function notation. Given that the

$\tan X = \dfrac{\sin X}{\cos X}$, write a statement to place the tan THETA in the variable TRIG.

_____

TRIG = SINF(THETA)/COSF(THETA)
    If your answer agrees with the one shown above, continue with the next frame. If your answer does not agree, return to frame 4.6 and review.

4.27   Another example of function notation using library function names might be:

$$Y = \text{SINF(SQRTF(LOGF(X(I) ** 2)))}$$

This is a three-deep nesting of functions, where the log function value is the argument for the square root function whose value is, in turn, the argument for the sine function.

The first computation executed by the computer in the above example would be
_____ .

X(I) ** 2

4.28 That example, Y = SINF(SQRTF(LOGF(X(I) ** 2))), further illustrates the fact that an argument can be any legal FORTRAN expression. The computer treats nested functions by starting with the innermost point and computing its way out. Thus, X(I) ** 2 is computed first, and its value is given to the log function whose result is the argument to the square root function; the final result becomes the value of Y.

The *entire* argument of the sine function shown above is (written out)
_____ .

(SQRTF(LOGF(X(I) ** 2)))
(Which is still a single quantity.)

4.29 Function notation is not limited to expressions appearing in arithmetic formula statements either. For example, IF (SINF(OMEGA * T))10,20,30 will tell the computer to compute the value of OMEGA * T, give that result to the sine function, and test the final result for negative, zero, or positive status.

EXERCISE 4.1

Solve the trigonometric formula shown below for all 100 angles in the ANGLE array, placing the answers in the Y array. The ANGLE values are all in *degrees* (57.29578 degrees per radian), and the library functions use radians as the proper dimension for their arguments.

$$y = \tan^{-1} (\sin^2 x + \tan^3 x)$$

given that $\quad \tan x = \dfrac{\sin x}{\cos x} \quad \tan^{-1} = \arctan \neq \dfrac{1}{\tan}$

4.30 Library functions represent only one type of function which may be used in FORTRAN programs. There are a total of four kinds of function subprograms listed below. If you are of the opinion that there are too many types, you are not alone; however, their individual merits will soon become clear.
1. Library functions
2. Built-in functions
3. Arithmetic statement functions
4. FORTRAN-written FUNCTION subprograms

4.31 The library functions as described in the preceding frames are a set of previously written programs available to your program at execution time, being called into action wherever their particular name appears in your program. In addition to the standard set, a library may have additional programs available.

4.32 Write a statement, using the appropriate function, to compute the square root of the sum of A squared and B squared. Place the result in HYPTNS.

HYPTNS = SQRTF(A ** 2 + B ** 2)

4.33 The question of the preceding frame demonstrates a typical use of a library function. Note that the argument is itself an expression, which is perfectly permissible. Incidentally, the use of SQRTF for computing square roots is more efficient than using the notation ** 0.5.

[true or false] In the answer shown above, the value of the expression A ** 2 + B ** 2 is computed before the function is enacted to compute the square root.

---

true
  Notice how this amends the hierarchy rules when function notation is used!

4.34 The *built-in* functions mentioned in frame 4.30 are also pre-written programs which are made available to your program by using their names in ordinary expressions. The principal difference between built-in and library functions is the way in which they are made available to a program.

[true or false] Built-in functions are used in function notation in the same way that library functions are. _____

true

4.35 The built-in functions are program segments which are placed right in your program wherever they are used. If you use the same built-in function more than once in a program, the actual subprogram segment appears each time. This type of subprogram is called an "open subprogram."

The _____ functions are examples of open subprograms.

built-in

4.36 The built-in functions are the only subprograms in the FORTRAN system which use this open subprogram approach. The other three types of functions are of the closed subprogram variety. This means that a library function, for example, appears only *once* regardless how many times it is used in a given program.

Library functions are examples of _____ subprograms.

closed

4.37 Both the library and built-in functions are previously written programs of general interest. The third type of function, the arithmetic statement function, is used where no library or built-in function is available. This type of function is defined by the programmer right in the program in which it is to be used.

4.38 These three types of functions are similar in many respects. They are called upon in the same way from a program (by the use of the appropriate name), their names are subject to the same rules and conventions (the fourth function type is different), and the argument(s) rules are the same.

[true or false] Since a function name is itself a legal expression, any of the above mentioned function types could be used as the argument of another function. _____

true

4.39 The library, built-in, and arithmetic statement functions are all named according to the same convention; the function name may have from four to seven alphanumeric characters, the first is alphabetic and the last is the letter F. It is the presence of the F which labels the name as a function.

[true or false] The name ARF is a legal function name according to the above definition. _____

false
    A function name must have at least four characters, including the F.

4.40 Although the library and built-in functions are already named, they and the arithmetic statement functions (named by the programmer) are all subject to the same set of rules. It should be noted that *variable names* which have more than four characters should not end in the letter F!

A variable name of four or more characters ending in F might be mistaken for a _____ name.

function

4.41   The following list contains a set of function names. Identify the legal ones with a plus sign and the illegal ones with a minus sign. Remember, they must have at least four but not more than seven alphanumeric characters, the first being alphabetic and the last F.

SINF	_____	FIRSTF	_____
OFF	_____	123456F	_____
FOFXF	_____	F! $\sqrt{\pi}$ $\int$?F	_____
FLOATF	_____	FUNCTION	_____

SINF	+	
OFF	−	(only three characters)
FOFXF	+	
FLOATF	+	
FIRSTF	+	
123456F	−	(does not begin with alphabetic)
F! $\sqrt{\pi}$ $\int$?F	−	(contains nonalphanumeric characters)
FUNCTION	−	(has too many characters)

4.42   The question of mode comes up with functions as well as variables and expressions. In the case of function subprograms, mode conventions have to be observed on two counts: the function value and the arguments. The mode of the function value is denoted by the function name, as defined in the following frame.

4.43   The computed value of the function must have a particular mode associated with it, since it is used in an expression with other quantities. Unfortunately, the mode convention for function names is different from that for variables, and confusion may result. If the *first* letter of a function name is X, the function *value* is treated as fixed-point; if the *first* letter of a function name is other than X the value is floating-point.

The function name LOGF (library function) indicates a _____ -point value for the function.

> floating
>   The letters I, J, K, L, M, and N do not denote fixed-point mode in library function names.

4.44   When inventing a name for an arithmetic statement function, be sure to observe the mode rule that the function's value will be treated as fixed-point only if the function name begins with X. Both the library and built-in function names have been assigned in line with this convention.

The function name XFIXF denotes a _____ -point value for the function.

> fixed

4.45 The argument or arguments of a function may be of either mode; that is, the name of the function itself does not imply that an argument is of a particular mode. When a function itself is programmed, the mode of any arguments is defined, and it is up to the user of a function to see that the argument supplied is of the correct mode.

All of the standard library functions utilize arguments of the _____-point mode.

floating

4.46 It should be pointed out that a function can only be used in an expression of the same mode as that of the function's name. The mode required for the *arguments,* however, does not have any bearing on the mode of the expression in which the function appears.

According to the above definitions, the statement $Y = A + B + FLOATF(I)$ is [legal or illegal] _____ .

legal

4.47 The following is a list of points with which you should be thoroughly familiar before continuing:

1. A function name appearing in a FORTRAN expression results in the execution of a program.
2. This program has been previously written.
3. One of these subprogram types is made available through a library.
4. A function is recognized by its name.
5. A function name has 4 to 7 characters, the last of which is F.
6. If a function name begins with X the function value is fixed-point; otherwise, it is floating-point.

EXERCISE 4.2

Identify the mode of the functions' values in the list below:

(*a*)	XACTF	(*d*)	INTGERF
(*b*)	NUMBERF	(*e*)	XCESSF
(*c*)	SIMPLEF		

4.48 The built-in functions, like the library functions, are automatically made available to any program which makes use of the appropriate name. The standard FORTRAN system (for all but 705 FORTRAN) contains twenty different built-in functions which will be explained in the next several frames with examples. Incidentally, these do not need to be committed to memory since they are written up in reference manuals, but a familiarity and working knowledge of these built-in functions will be helpful in their use.

4.49 One of the simplest of the built-in functions will provide the *absolute value* of a quantity. This means that the value of the function will be the positive magnitude of the argument, regardless of the original sign of the argument quantity. The function is ABSF (or XABSF for fixed-point use).

By the above definition, the value of the expression ABSF(X) will always be (sign) _____ .

> positive (plus)

4.50 Important note: This function, like every other function, does nothing to the argument itself. For example, the statement Y = ABSF(A) uses the value of A to determine the value of the function, but the value of A remains intact in its original form.

If A in the above example has a value of -1.234, the value of Y after execution would be _____ .

> $+1.234$

4.51 Thus you can see that the only operation performed by the ABSF or XABSF functions is to set the sign of the argument value (but not the argument itself) to be positive. This can be a valuable function, however simple it may seem, as in the example SQRTF(ABSF(X)), which assures that the argument to the square root function is a positive quantity (which it indeed must be).

If you needed the absolute value of the variable NUMBER you would write the expression _____ .

> XABSF(NUMBER)
> The XABSF function must be used, since it is designed to handle fixed-point arguments.

4.52 This last question brings up an important point: these built-in functions are designed to handle arguments of a particular mode. The mode of the argument does not necessarily agree with the mode of the function, but in the case of XABSF it does happen to agree, and, in fact, must be written that way.

[true or false] The statement Y = ABSF(NUMBER) is legal. _____

> false
> ABSF is the name used with floating-point arguments *only*.

EXERCISE 4.3

Write a statement which will direct the computer to statement 10 if the absolute value of X is greater than 0.001 or go to statement 100 if the absolute value of X is less than or equal to that quantity.

4.53 Another built-in function performs a very useful operation: selecting the largest quantity of a set of quantities. That is, it determines the algebraically largest quantity; for example, it would determine that $+1.0$ is larger than -2.0. This function is called by four names, depending on the modes of the function value and the arguments.

Name	Mode of Function	Mode of Arguments	Example
MAX1F	Floating	Floating	MAX1F(A,B,C)
XMAX1F	Fixed	Floating	XMAX1F(A,B,C)
MAX0F	Floating	Fixed	MAX0F(I,J,K)
XMAX0F	Fixed	Fixed	XMAX0F(I,J,K)

4.54 These four versions of the same function give all the possible combinations of mode required (however, all the arguments must be of the same mode in a given version). Thus, for example, if you want the floating-point value which is the largest of A, B, or C, you would use the first form: MAX1F(A,B,C). Note that, when a function has more than one argument, they must be separated by commas.

The two forms of this function which give a *value* of the same mode as its *arguments* are _____ and _____ .

> MAX1F, XMAX0F
> These are the most common uses; the other two combinations are special-purpose.

4.55 Incidentally, this is a rarity among functions; there is no set amount of arguments that you may have. Thus you can determine the maximum value of two quantities, ten quantities, or as many as you care to write in the argument list. (Nearly all functions have a set number of arguments which must be rigidly observed.)

[true or false] The expression MAX1F(A(I), I = 1, 1000) is legal.

> false
> Handy as it looks, the self-indexed form is only available to input or output lists.

4.56 It is important that you use the correct name out of the four possibilities. If you use XMAX1F, for example, it will treat the arguments as floating-point quantities while finding the maximum, then convert that value to fixed-point for the value of the function; therefore, this form is used in a fixed-point expression and contains floating-point arguments.

If A, B, and C have the values 1., 3., and 2. respectively, the value of MAX1F(A,B,C) is _____ .

4.57 In general then, the maximum function, in one of its four forms, searches the values of the variable-length list of arguments for the largest value which in turn becomes the value of the function. If either MAX0F or XMAX1F is used, the mode of the result is converted to the opposite mode.

[true or false] The statements Y = MAX0F(I,J) and Y = XMAX0F(I,J) give identical results. _____

4.58 The two statements, Y = MAX0F(I,J) and Y = XMAX0F(I,J), of this preceding question are identical in the result obtained for Y. The first case yields a floating-point version of the larger of I and J through the function process, while the second case involves a function value that is fixed-point which is converted by the natural action of arithmetic formula statements (when the modes across the equals sign are different).

If the variables A, B, and C have the values 1., 3., and 2. respectively, XMAX1F(A,B,C) will have the value _____ .

EXERCISE 4.4

Given that X is a positive quantity write a statement using MAX1F to fulfill the following conditions:

$$y = x^2 \quad \text{if } x \text{ is greater than 5.0}$$
$$y = 25.0 \quad \text{if } x \text{ is less than or equal to 5.0}$$

4.59 Another built-in function provides four forms of similar combinations to determine the minimum of a set of quantities. The rules for using this function are exactly the same as those for the maximum function. The following frame will show the four forms with examples.

Name	Mode of Function	Mode of Argument	Example
MIN1F	Floating	Floating	MIN1F(A,B,C)
XMIN1F	Fixed	Floating	XMIN1F(A,B,C)
MIN0F	Floating	Fixed	MIN0F(I,J,K)
XMIN0F	Fixed	Fixed	XMIN0F(I,J,K)

4.60 The following are some examples of the ten functions described so far:

INDEX = XMAX1F(X,Y,Z) + XMIN1F(ABSF(A),ABSF(B),ABSF(C))
IF (ABSF(MAX1F(P,Q,R,S) − 1,0))10,20,30
K = XMIN0F(XABSF(I,J),XABSF(XMIN1F(A,B)),0)
SMALL = MIN1F(MIN0F(I,J,K,L,M),MAX0F(N,0,XMAX0F(LOW,LESS,L)))

The complete argument (written out) of the MIN0F in the last example above is _____ .

> (I,J,K,L,M)

EXERCISE 4.5

Write a *single* statement that will find the largest number of I1,I2, I3, and I4, then find the largest number of J1, J2, J3, and J4, and, finally, place the smaller of these two maximums in the floating-point variable A.

4.61 A built-in function is available to change the mode of a *single* argument; the value of this function is then the argument's value in the opposite mode. The form FLOATF (argument) is used to convert from fixed-to floating-point; the form XFIXF (argument) is used for the opposite conversion.

In which mode do you think the *argument* of XFIXF should be? _____

> floating-point
> (This function converts from floating-point to fixed-point.)

4.62 As the last question implies, the FLOATF and XFIXF forms must have arguments of opposite mode to the name of the function; thus, FLOATF(N) and XFIXF(A) would be legal uses of these functions, but the form FLOATF(A) or XFIXF(K) would yield meaningless numbers.

[yes or no] Is there any difference in the result of the statements Y = K and Y = FLOATF(K)? _____

> no
> Either form will produce the floating-point value of K for the variable Y.

4.63 This last question may raise some doubt about the usefulness of the FLOATF and XFIXF functions. Actually, they turn out to be very useful when a quantity of one mode is used in an expression of another mode, as in Y = A+B+FLOATF(K), saving the extra step of converting K in another statement.

[yes or no] Is there any difference in the results of the statements K = N and
K = XFIXF(FLOATF(N))? _____

4.64　The XFIXF form can hold some surprises for you if you forget that the
fixed-point mode contains only *integers* and the conversion from floating-point
involves dropping (*not* rounding) the fraction part. Thus, XFIXF(1.9999999) has
a value of 1 (fixed-point, truncated).

If X has a value of 3.0, the value of Y after executing

$$Y = FLOATF(XFIXF(X/2.0))$$

would be _____ .

4.65　This action of dropping the fractional part of a floating-point quantity
and then restoring the number to floating-point mode is the function of a type
called INTF(argument). In other words, INTF(X/2.0) has the same value (1.0) as
FLOATF(XFIXF(X/2.0)), performing the equivalent operations in a single
function.

The integer function INTF has a value in the _____-point mode.

4.66　A companion form for INTF is the function XINTF, which also has
a floating-point argument, but leaves the converted number in the fixed-point
mode. In other words XINTF is just XFIXF by another name.

If the variable X has a value of 11.9975, the value of the expression XINTF(X)
is _____ .

4.67　Let's look at an example of the use of the truncation function. Suppose
you wished to create an index K which would have the value 1 if X fell between
0. and 5.0, 2 if X were between 5.0 and 10.0, 3 if X were between 10.0 and 15.0,
etc. An expression such as K = XINTF(X/5.0) + 1 would do the trick.

If X had a value of 23.0 in the statement shown above, K would have a value of _____ .

4.68 Another built-in function set will perform the modulo operation (residue, or remaindering). That is, a division of two quantities is carried out and the integer part is discarded and the remainder is the result. Thus, 5 modulo 2 is computed by dividing 5 by 2 and keeping the remainder (5/2 is 2 with a residue of 1) so that 5 modulo 2 is 1. Some other examples: 15 modulo 10 is 5, 12 modulo 2 is 0, 7 modulo 3 is 1.

The value of 11 modulo 5 is _____ .

4.69 The function to perform the modulo arithmetic is in two forms: MODF and XMODF, which have values in floating-point and fixed-point modes, respectively. Incidentally, their arguments agree in mode with the mode of the function value. Both forms use exactly *two* arguments.

[true or false] The expression MODF(A,B) is legitimate. _____

4.70 Both forms perform the modulo arithmetic in such a way that the result will be *(first argument) modulo (second argument),* or in our example, MODF(A,B), the computer would compute A modulo B. Similarly, in the fixed-point version, XMODF(I,J) performs I modulo J.

If I has a value of 9 and J a value of 2, the expression XMODF(I,J) will have a value of _____ .

4.71 An interesting use of the XMODF function is to determine if an integer is odd or even. One property of a number modulo 2 is the fact that this always yields a value of 0 or 1. In fact, if the number is *odd* the modulo operation will give a value of 1; if the number is *even* the modulo operation will yield a 0.

The statement IF (XMODF(K,2))10,20,10 will send the computer to statement 20 if K is an _____ number.

4.72 A built-in function is available to transfer the algebraic sign from one quantity to another. The function SIGNF(argument 1, argument 2) will have as its value the absolute magnitude of the first argument times the algebraic sign of the second argument. (Both arguments are floating-point.)

4.73 This function has its counterpart in the fixed-point form as XSIGNF(arg. 1, arg. 2), which performs the same function for fixed-point quantities. Thus, for example, SIGNF(-1.5, 2.3) would equal $+1.5$ after execution, while SIGNF-($-1.$, $-5.$) would have the value -1.

If L and M both have the value -10, the expression XSIGNF(L,M) will equal _____ .

-10

4.74 The last of the built-in functions is the DIMF and XDIMF forms of the diminish function. This function has exactly two arguments, and its value, in either mode used, is the *first argument* minus the algebraically smaller of the *two arguments,* giving either a zero or a positive difference for the result.

4.75 The DIMF and XDIMF functions behave as follows:

DIMF(4.,3.) equals 1.0
DIMF(4.3,6.7) equals 0.0

Similarly

XDIMF(4,3) equals 1
XDIMF(4,8) equals 0

The expression XDIMF(6,2) will equal _____ .

4

This has been a rather exhaustive (and perhaps exhausting) exposition of the built-in function set available with FORTRAN. The following frames will present summaries of the function types with information concerning number and mode of arguments, mode of function value, etc.

4.76

Absolute Value Function

Name	Number of arguments	Mode of argument	Mode of function	Example
ABSF	1	Floating	Floating	ABSF(X ** 2 $-$ 1.0)
XABSF	1	Fixed	Fixed	XABSF(I $-$ L)

4.77

Maximum Value Function

Name	Number of arguments	Mode of argument	Mode of function	Example
MAX1F	≥ 2	Floating	Floating	MAX1F(X,Y,Z)
XMAX1F	≥ 2	Floating	Fixed	XMAX1F(A(I),B,2.)
MAX0F	≥ 2	Fixed	Floating	MAX0F(N(K),L,M)
XMAX0F	≥ 2	Fixed	Fixed	XMAX0F(MI,LA)

4.78

Minimum Value Function

Name	Number of arguments	Mode of argument	Mode of function	Example
MIN1F	≥ 2	Floating	Floating	MIN1F(X,Y,Z)
XMIN1F	≥ 2	Floating	Fixed	XMIN1F(A(I),B,2.)
MIN0F	≥ 2	Fixed	Floating	MIN0F(N(K),L,M)
XMIN0F	≥ 2	Fixed	Fixed	XMIN0F(MI,LA)

4.79

Mode Conversion and Truncation Functions

Name	Number of arguments	Mode of argument	Mode of function	Example
FLOATF	1	Fixed	Floating	FLOATF(INDEX)
XFIXF	1	Floating	Fixed	XFIXF(ALPHA)
INTF	1	Floating	Floating	INTF(VALUE)
XINTF	1	Floating	Fixed	XINTF(ALPHA)

4.80

Modulo (Remaindering) Function

Name	Number of arguments	Mode of argument	Mode of function	Example
MODF	2	Floating	Floating	MODF(X,2.0)
XMODF	2	Fixed	Fixed	XMODF(K,2)

Additional Functions

Name	Number of arguments	Mode of argument	Mode of function	Example
SIGNF	2	Floating	Floating	SIGNF(A,B)
XSIGNF	2	Fixed	Fixed	XSIGNF(L,M)
DIMF	2	Floating	Floating	DIMF(W,Z)
XDIMF	2	Fixed	Fixed	XDIMF(K,KK)

4.82   The two function types discussed so far in this chapter are both of the previously written variety; that is, they already exist as you read this text, with their own special names and function programs. The next type of function which will be explained will be written by a programmer for his own use with function notation.

4.83   The third type of function is the arithmetic statement function. Any functional relationship which can be expressed in a *single expression* can be applied to an arithmetic statement function. To show a trivial example, suppose you desired a function which would sum up its three arguments.

$$SUMF(A,B,C) = A + B + C$$

The three arguments in the example above are _____ , _____ , and _____ .

A, B, C

4.84   Every arithmetic statement function is defined by a single statement which consists of the selected name with its arguments followed by an equals sign and followed in turn by the FORTRAN expression which defines the desired functional relationship. The example $SUMF(A,B,C) = A + B + C$ is such a statement.

The name of the function defined by $SUMF(A,B,C) = A + B + C$ is _____ .

SUMF

4.85   The single statement which defines the arithmetic statement function's relationships is called a "function defining statement." When such a statement appears in a program, the indicated operations will be performed wherever the function's *name* appears in an expression elsewhere in that program.

[true or false] The statement $SUMF(A,B,C) = A + B + C$ is a function defining statement. _____

true

4.86   In other words, if you write the statement SUMF(A,B,C) = A+B+C (a function defining statement) in your program, you can use this function simply by writing its name in an expression elsewhere in the program as in the example Y = SUMF(X,Y,Z)/SUMF(P,Q,R). X, Y, and Z (and P, Q, and R) will be operated on in the manner prescribed by the arguments in the function defining statement.

If X, Y, and Z have the values 1., 3., and 2. respectively, the value of SUMF(X,Y,Z) is _____ .

6.0

4.87   The function defining statement contains argument variables both with the function name and also in the expression on the right of the equals sign. When that function *name* then appears in an expression elsewhere in the program, whatever quantities are given there as arguments will be used in the manner prescribed by the function defining statement.

The expression FIRSTF(A,B) will provide the values of _____ and _____ to the subprogram called FIRSTF.

A, B

4.88   The variables listed as arguments in the *function defining statement,* then, are *dummy arguments,* meaning that they are not variables in the usual sense, but are used to show what is to be done with the values of the *actual arguments* as indicated in the function notation elsewhere in the program.

Given the statement SUMF(A,B,C) = A+B+C, the expression SUMF(2.,2.,2.) has a value of _____ .

6.
A, B, and C are dummy arguments; the 2.'s are actual arguments.

4.89   Any functional relationship which can be expressed in a single expression can be expressed in the arithmetic statement function form. The expression on the right of the function defining statement may contain variables (unsubscripted), constants, and even other function names.

[true or false] The statement CUTOFF(X) = A(I) ** 2+X(I) ** 2 is a legal function defining statement. _____

false
    Subscripted variables are not permitted in the expression of a function defining statement.

4.90   The function defining statement's expression may make use of ordinary variables in addition to the dummy argument variables listed on the left. When this is the case, these ordinary variables will contribute their current values to the computation of the function, while, of course, the argument values will be supplied by the statement which called on the function.

In the statement SOMEF(X) = A * X ** 2 the expression contains an argument (dummy) variable _____ and an ordinary variable _____ .

X, A

4.91 The example SOMEF(X) = A * X ** 2 demonstrates an expression containing an argument variable and an ordinary variable. A statement elsewhere in the program such as Y = SOMEF(Z) will cause this function to be computed using the current value of A, and the value of Z is used where X appears in the definition.

Every statement containing the name SOMEF will call upon the function defined above, specifying an argument value which will be treated like the variable _____ in the definition.

X

4.92 All function defining statements must come first in your program, before *every* other statement. You see, this statement is not executed in the same sense that an ordinary arithmetic formula statement is; it appears only once in the program, but its indicated operations are carried out each time its name appears in an expression, and control remains with the statement which called upon the function.

4.93 Since the arithmetic statement function is written by a programmer for his special application, it follows that he must also assign a name to that function. The name must conform to the usual function-naming convention: 4 to 7 alphanumeric characters, first alphabetic, last F; if the first letter is X, the function value will be treated as fixed-point.

[true or false] The names ANYOLDF, SCOFF, XACTF, and ONOFF are all legal floating-point function names. _____

false
    XACTF has a fixed-point value.

4.94 Let's look at a practical example: suppose you need to compute the expression $\sqrt{x^2 + y^2}$ several times with different values for the parameters. Rather than repeat this expression in each statement that needs it, you can define a function called, say, POLARF(X, Y) which can be used by name in each expression that requires it. A suitable function defining statement would be POLARF(X, Y) = SQRTF(X ** 2 + Y ** 2).

Using the above definition, the value of POLARF(3., 4.) would be _____.

5.

4.95 Write a function defining statement using the name ROOTF(A, B, C) that will solve the expression $\dfrac{-b + \sqrt{b^2 - 4ac}}{2a}$. _____

ROOTF(A, B, C) = (−B + SQRTF(B ** 2 − 4. * A * C))/(2. * A)
   All parentheses are necessary.
   If your answer agrees with the one shown, skip to Exercise 4.6 on page 163. If you did not get the correct answer, continue with the next frame (unless you just omitted some parentheses in the expression).

4.96 Given the relation $\dfrac{-b + \sqrt{b^2 - 4ac}}{2a}$, and the potential name of the function, ROOTF, the writing of the function defining statement should be a simple matter of filling in the blanks: name, arguments, equals sign, and expression (the library SQRTF is permitted in the expression of a function defining statement).

Write a function defining statement for DISCRMF(A, B, C) to compute the square root in the above expression. _____

DISCRMF(A, B, C) = SQRTF(B ** 2 − 4. * A * C)

4.97 The basic idea of these arithmetic statement functions is to program a commonly used set of operations in a form that can be used with function notation throughout the program. For example, a statement such as IF (DISCRMF-(X, Y, Z))10,20,30 used in a program containing the above definition will carry out those indicated operations without rewriting them, which will be the case as many times as you wish to use it.

[true or false] A function defining statement must be the first statement in the program. _____

true

4.98 Try another case. Write a function defining statement for a function called TRIGF which will compute the square root of the sine of the first argument and multiply this by the second argument. (Use THETA and PHI for the argument variables.) _____

TRIGF(THETA,PHI) = SQRTF(SINF(THETA)) * PHI
   If your answer agrees with the one shown, do Exercise 4.6. If your answer is wrong, better go back to frame 4.83 and read carefully the material on arithmetic statement functions.

EXERCISE 4.6

Write a function defining statement to compute the expression $\tan^{-1}\left(\frac{x}{y}\right)$ where $\tan^{-1}$ signifies arctangent. Use the name ANGLEF.

4.99 You have now become familiar with three of the four types of functions used in FORTRAN programs: the library, built-in, and arithmetic statement functions. The first two types are available automatically and consist of a specific set of prewritten programs. The third type is written for a particular program's use by the programmer himself.

Since the name SOMEF does not belong to the set of library or built-in functions, it must be an _____ _____ function.

arithmetic statement

4.100 Most of the function usage can be satisfied by these three function types. Occasionally, however, a function is needed that is not in the library or built-in packages and also cannot be expressed in a single expression, as required for the arithmetic statement functions. For these cases, FORTRAN-written subprograms are used.

[true or false] Arithmetic statement functions can only be used where the function's value can be defined in a single function defining statement. _____

true

4.101 The FORTRAN-written subprogram fulfills the same purpose that the arithmetic statement function does, except that this type of function permits as many statements as necessary to fully define the functional relationship for which the function is being written.

[true or false] The fourth type of function, the FORTRAN-written subprogram, permits only one statement in the function definition. _____

false
  As many statements as needed are permitted.

4.102 The FORTRAN-written subprograms exist in two forms: the FUNCTION subprogram and the SUBROUTINE subprogram. To provide a mental picture of the overall subprogram setup, a diagram is shown below.

	Functions		Subroutine
Library	Arithmetic statement		SUBROUTINE
Built-in	FUNCTION		

The FORTRAN-written version of the function family is called a _____ subprogram.

4.103 The FUNCTION subprogram (the capital letters are used intentionally to distinguish this function type) is itself a *complete* program; that is, it is written separate from any program which uses it and even has its own END statement, which is used for all programs to signify the last statement in the program.

When a FUNCTION subprogram is written with another program, at least _____ END statements are needed.

two
    One each for the FUNCTION subprogram and the other program.

4.104 The FUNCTION subprogram is a completely separate segment of programming from that program which makes use of the function. This type of subprogramming enables you to write a complete *set* of statements which will only be executed if another program makes reference to the chosen name of the FUNCTION.

[true or false] The FUNCTION is essentially the same in use as the other three types of functions. _____

true

4.105 The FUNCTION subprogram, then, is used like a library function; it is a previously written program which is executed wherever its name appears in *another* program. In other words, if you find you need a function and it is not available in the library, you can write it yourself with FORTRAN statements in FUNCTION form.

[true or false] The FUNCTION subprogram is written completely in FORTRAN language. _____

true

4.106 The FUNCTION programs are distinguished from ordinary programs by the very first statement in the program. A special statement is used, beginning with the word FUNCTION followed by its name, an open parenthesis, a list of "dummy" arguments, and a closing parenthesis: e.g., FUNCTION NAME (ARG1,ARG2,ARG3).

The FUNCTION statement shown above must be the _____ statement in the FUNCTION program.

first

4.107 Following the FUNCTION statement you may write any combination of statements you wish to properly define the functional relationship between the argument quantities and the single result which becomes the value of the function.

A program beginning with the statement FUNCTION THING(A, B, C) is a _____ subprogram.

4.108 In addition to identifying a program as a FUNCTION, the FUNCTION statement itself fulfills two purposes: it defines the name of the FUNCTION, and also indicates, through the list of dummy argument variables, the quantities whose values are to be supplied by the program which uses the FUNCTION.

The FUNCTION statement defines the _____ of the FUNCTION.

4.109 Functions of this fourth type have different naming rules than the other three function types; the name can have from 1 to 6 alphanumeric characters, the first of which must be alphabetic and the last of which must *not* be the letter F. In other words, the fourth function type has the same naming rules as ordinary variables.

[true or false] The name A would be a legal FUNCTION name. _____

4.110 To compare the naming rules: the library, built-in, and arithmetic statement functions are all named with 4 to 7 character names, the first of which is alphabetic and the last of which is F; the FUNCTION subprogram is named with 1 to 6 characters like any ordinary variable.

[true or false] The name FIRSTF would be a suitable FUNCTION name. _____

4.111 You will remember that the mode of the first three function types is determined by the name. If the name begins with the letter X, the mode of the function value is fixed-point; otherwise, the mode is floating-point. The FUNCTION mode, however, is determined the same as is the mode of an ordinary variable. If the first letter is I, J, K, L, M, or N, the mode is fixed-point; otherwise, the mode is floating-point.

The FUNCTION name JUNK belongs to the _____ point mode.

4.112   Classify the following function names with respect to type of function
and the mode of the function's value:

Name	Type	Mode
XFOFX	_____	_____
EXPF	_____	_____
XINTF	_____	_____
LAMBDA	_____	_____

4.113   [true or false] Using the functions described above, the expression
XFOFX(A,X) * XINTF(X) is legal. _____

4.114   So far, then, you have seen that you can write your own FUNCTION
subprograms to be used by other programs of yours in exactly the same manner
that you use the library and other functions. Unlike the arithmetic statement
functions, however, the FUNCTION is a separate program segment headed by
the FUNCTION statement, terminated by its own END statement, and containing
statements defining the function.

4.115   The FUNCTION statement which heads the FUNCTION subprogram
contains the name you have chosen for the FUNCTION and also contains the list
of dummy variables whose values are to be supplied to the program by the
program which uses the FUNCTION. The name is chosen by the same rules
applied to variables.

[true or false] The statement FUNCTION ABCDEFG(X, Y, Z) is valid.
_____

4.116   All FUNCTION subprograms use a special statement to tell the computer to return to the program which called on the FUNCTION and pick up where it left off. When the FUNCTION subprogram has finished its task of computing its particular value, the RETURN statement (consisting of the word RETURN) signals the computer to go back to the other program.

The RETURN statement sends the control back to the program which used the _____ of the FUNCTION.

4.117   This brings the total of new statements in this chapter to *two:* the FUNCTION statement and the RETURN statement. The RETURN statement is used in a subprogram where you might use a STOP in a regular program: that is, as the last statement to be *executed* (remember, the END statement is actually last).

The three statement types that must be included in every FUNCTION are FUNCTION, END, and _____ .

4.118   One other statement is required of every FUNCTION subprogram: an arithmetic formula statement which sets the *name* of the FUNCTION equal to the final computed result, treating the name as an ordinary variable (using *only* the name, without any parentheses or arguments). This may be placed anywhere in the program, although it often comes just before the RETURN statement, and it links the result with the other program. Examples of this will be shown in future frames.

4.119   Now that the general framework has been defined, we can study an example of a FUNCTION program and how it is used by another program. The program on the following page will provide as its value the *sum* of the array specified as its first argument, considering the array to be of length defined by the second argument.

4.120   Sample program segments:

```
            FUNCTION SUM(A,N)
            (Specification statement not yet covered)
            SUM = A(1)
            DO 10 I = 2,N
        10  SUM = SUM + A(I)
            RETURN
            END
```

4.121   The first statement in the subprogram of frame 4.120 is, of course, the FUNCTION statement, defining the chosen name and the dummy arguments. The second statement is one which will be covered later. The actual program is defined in the next three statements: initialize the SUM and loop to keep adding successive numbers in the array into SUM. (Notice that the FUNCTION name, SUM, is treated like a variable.) When the loop is completed, the RETURN will take the computer back to whatever program has used the FUNCTION.

[true or false] The sample program would not be complete without the END statement: _____ .

> true
> (All programs, even subprograms, require an END statement.)

4.122   The example of frame 4.120 demonstrates another feature of FUNC-TION subprograms that is not available with the other types: the argument quantities may be *arrays* (the argument, for example, of the SINF must be a *single* quantity). You must be careful to treat the argument quantities accordingly, however!

In this example, the program headed by FUNCTION SUM(A,N) treated the argument named _____ as an array.

> A

4.123   It is important to understand that the arguments as specified in the FUNCTION statement are *dummy* variables. This means that their names are used in the subprogram without definition of value, and the value used for any particular execution will be supplied by the statement in the other program. For instance, in the above example, the variable A was one of the dummy variables, and anywhere the name A appeared in the FUNCTION the value of the *first* argument in the other program would be used, even if its name were not A.

4.124   Sample program segments:

	FUNCTION SUM (A,N)	(Some pertinent program statements)
	(Specification statement)	Y = SUM(BLOCK,KOUNT)
	SUM = A(1)	(Continuation of program)
	DO 10 I = 2,N	END
10	SUM = SUM + A(I)	
	RETURN	
	END	

4.125   Frame 4.124 shows *two* programs; the one on the left is the same FUNCTION SUM(A,N) described before. The one on the right is part of another program which uses SUM. Notice that the other program uses the arguments

BLOCK and KOUNT. This means that BLOCK and KOUNT will be used by the FUNCTION wherever the names A and N appear; A and N are just dummies (notice that the modes agree!).

[true or false] Both programs in frame 4.124 must be terminated by END statements as shown. _____

true

4.126 Suppose the other program in that example had another statement such as Z = SUM(VECTOR,K). This simply means that the FUNCTION called SUM would be executed again, this time using the values of VECTOR and K where the dummy names A and N appear in the FUNCTION.

The statement in the other program which uses the FUNCTION name shown above must contain exactly _____ arguments.

two

4.127 When you write a FUNCTION subprogram and use it in various other programs with statements containing its name, make sure that you specify the same number of arguments in both places (the FUNCTION statement and the expression in the other program). Also, make certain that the *mode* agrees with what is expected.

[true or false] The statement Y = SUM(X,Y) would be legal for the FUNCTION just described. _____

false
   The second argument must be fixed-point.

4.128 Since subprograms of the FUNCTION type are written as separate programs from the program that makes use of them, there is no correlation of variable names and statement numbers between the programs. The only way a FUNCTION can make use of a quantity in another program is through the dummy arguments.

The statement Y = SUM(X,N) provides the subprogram SUM with the values of _____ and _____ .

X, N

4.129 Thus, a program and an associated subprogram can both use the same variable names and statement numbers without any conflict. The only time a variable in a subprogram has a value related to another program is when that subprogram variable is a dummy argument.

A program headed by the statement FUNCTION SQUARE(X,Y) utilizes a total of _____ quantities from the program which uses the FUNCTION.

two

4.130   Here are some check points in the writing and using of FUNCTION subprograms:

1. Choose a name that is of the correct mode and does not end in F (1 to 6 letters in all).
2. Make certain that all the information needed in the FUNCTION is included in the list of arguments.
3. Be sure that the FUNCTION has the proper FUNCTION, RE-TURN, and END statements.
4. Include a statement in the FUNCTION that sets its name equal to the desired result.
5. The FUNCTION name should be used in an expression of the same mode.
6. The arguments listed in the other program must agree in number and mode with the FUNCTION statement.

4.131   Using the FUNCTION SUM(A,N) as described on page 168, the statement Y = SUM(X,3)/SUM(Z,4) would result in a value of _____ for Y if the X array contained the numbers 4., 3., and 5., and the Z array contained the values 1., 2., 0., and 1.

3.
   If your answer agrees with the one given, skip to Exercise 4.7 on page 171. If you did not arrive at the correct answer, continue with the next frame.

4.132   The FUNCTION SUM(A,N) performed the task of adding the N quantities in the A array, giving the sum as the value of the FUNCTION. There-fore, the statement Y = SUM(X,3)/SUM(Z,4) is simply a statement which uses this FUNCTION twice and divides the two results.

When the expression SUM(X,3) is used, the value 3 is used in the FUNCTION where the variable _____ appeared.

N

4.133   Given that the X array contained the three values 4., 3., and 5., and that the Z array contained the four values 1., 2., 0., and 1., you could tell by adding them in your head that the expression SUM(X,3)/SUM(Z,4) is nothing more than 12. divided by 4., giving the result of 3. for the variable Y.

If the third number in the X array had been 9., the value of the expression above would have been _____ .

4.

4.134 Try a similar question. Using the same FUNCTION SUM(A,N) and given that the B array contains the integers 1. through 5. and the C array contains the integers 2. through 5., and K equals 5, what is the value of the expression SUM(B,K)–SUM(C,K-1)? _____

1.

If you answered this question correctly, you are probably getting the hang of the FUNCTION writing and usage. If not, return to frame 4.101 and review the material on FUNCTION subprograms. If you do feel confident of this material, do Exercise 4.7.

EXERCISE 4.7

Write a complete FUNCTION subprogram to find the algebraically smallest quantity in an array of 1000 or less values. The FUNCTION is to be called SMALL, and it will have two arguments: the dummy array name and a fixed-point variable telling how many numbers in the array. The answer will, of course, be made the value of the function.

4.135 The second type of subprogram, the SUBROUTINE which was mentioned earlier in this chapter, is similar to the FUNCTION in many respects; the naming rules are the same, they both require a RETURN statement and an END statement, and they both contain the same sort of dummy argument variables. Here the similarity ends, as will be explained in the next several frames.

4.136 Like the FUNCTION, the SUBROUTINE is also a set of commonly used operations grouped in subprogram form to be used again and again without rewriting, but it does not restrict itself to a single value for the result, as does the FUNCTION. In fact, a SUBROUTINE can be used for almost any operation with as many results as desired.

A SUBROUTINE, being a complete program segment, requires an _____ statement as the last statement.

END

4.137 The FUNCTION has a single value for its result which becomes the value of the FUNCTION name in the expression in which the name is used. Since the SUBROUTINE does not have just a single result, the manner in which the SUBROUTINE is called into action is different from the FUNCTION.

In the statement K = NAME(L,M,N) * I + J the value of the FUNCTION will replace the name _____ in computing the expression.

NAME

4.138 As the last question illustrates, the FUNCTION is called into action by mentioning its name in an expression. The SUBROUTINE is called by a special statement, the CALL statement, which consists of the word CALL followed by the name of the subprogram and its parenthesized list of arguments.

[true or false] By the above definition, the statement CALL MATMPY(A,B,N) is legal. _____

true

4.139 Remember, the name of a SUBROUTINE is chosen by the same rules as those of the FUNCTION subprogram. They may have 1 to 6 alphanumeric characters, the first of which must be alphabetic and the last of which must not be F. Unlike the FUNCTION, however, there is no mode associated with the SUBROUTINE name.

In the statement CALL MATMPY(A,B,N) the SUBROUTINE name is

_____ .

MATMPY

4.140 A programmer usually selects the SUBROUTINE name in a meaningful fashion. For example, the name MATMPY might be aptly applied to a SUBROUTINE which computed the product of two matrices. Since there is no numeric value associated with the name (as with a FUNCTION) there is no concern about mode.

If you want to make use of a SUBROUTINE in your program, you must use a _____ statement.

CALL

4.141 The SUBROUTINE itself is constructed with FORTRAN statements. You may use any sort of statement combinations you wish to perform the desired operations. Since the SUBROUTINE is a separate subprogram the variables and statement numbers do not relate to any other program (except the dummy argument variables).

A statement such as GO TO 15 in a subprogram requires that the subprogram have a statement numbered _____ .

4.142 The SUBROUTINE subprogram must begin with a special statement, like the FUNCTION statement. This statement consists of the word SUBROU-TINE followed by the subprogram name and its parenthesized list of dummy argument variables, as, for example, SUBROUTINE ORDER(X,Y,N).

The name of the subprogram defined in the statement above is _____ .

4.143 The SUBROUTINE subprogram must be headed by an appropriate SUBROUTINE statement as described in the previous frame; it must also end its execution with a RETURN statement, which, like the FUNCTION program, directs the computer back to the statement which called the subprogram in another program.

A SUBROUTINE, like a FUNCTION, must end its execution with a _____ statement.

4.144 Naturally the *last* statement in a SUBROUTINE subprogram must be an END statement. The END statement is the one which sets off program segments as complete main programs or subprograms. The next frame demon-strates a SUBROUTINE subprogram and a program which calls upon it. The object of the subprogram is to simply copy one array directly into another.

4.145 Sample program segments:

```
SUBROUTINE COPY (A,B,N)            (Some pertinent statements)
(Specification statement not yet covered)   CALL COPY (X,Y,K)
    DO 10 I = 1, N                 (Continue on)
10  B(I) = A(I)                    END
    RETURN
    END
```

4.146 The program on the above right is an ordinary main program which eventually executes a statement that will bring the SUBROUTINE into action (CALL COPY(X,Y,K)) telling the COPY subprogram to copy the X array into the Y array, K numbers long. The program on the left is the SUBROUTINE COPY (A,B,N) which defines the operations performed on the dummy arguments A, B, and N such that a DO loop is executed N times to copy the first given array into the second.

4.147 The example (in frame 4.145) demonstrates that the SUBROUTINE not only receives information from the arguments, but also defines the value of some of the arguments. This is the way in which the desired results are given back to the program which called on the SUBROUTINE. Thus the argument list becomes a two-way street.

In this example, the *dummy* argument (array) called ＿＿＿＿＿ had its value defined in the subprogram.

> B
>   B is the *dummy* argument in the SUBROUTINE; Y was the actual argument in the calling program.

4.148 A SUBROUTINE subprogram (or a FUNCTION, too, for that matter) can call upon another subprogram of any kind: library functions, built-in functions, arithmetic statement functions, or other SUBROUTINE or FUNCTION subprograms written in this subprogram form.

[true or false] The SQRTF can be used in any SUBROUTINE subprogram.

＿＿＿＿＿

> true

4.149 Subprograms can call on other subprograms to any desired number of levels. The RETURN statement or its equivalent will always send the computer back to the program which called on the subprogram, so you are assured that control will eventually get back to your main program.

If a main program calls upon a SUBROUTINE which in turn calls upon a FUNCTION, the RETURN statement in the FUNCTION will send the computer back to the (main or SUBROUTINE) ＿＿＿＿＿ program.

> SUBROUTINE
>   The RETURN statement always takes the computer back to the next program in sequence.)

4.150 A SUBROUTINE can be used for a large variety of jobs: sorting arrays, matrix manipulation, input or output, polynomial operations, etc. You should use a SUBROUTINE wherever you encounter this general type of operation and need to perform it more than once in a given program. The following frame will show a main program that reads an array from cards and calls on a SUBROUTINE to sort the array in algebraic order.

4.151 Sample program segments:

```
      READ 1,N,(A(I), I = 1, N)         SUBROUTINE ORDER (A,N)
  1   FORMAT (I5/(6F12.4))              K = N−1
      CALL ORDER(A,N)                   DO 10 I = 1,K
      PRINT 2,(A(I),I = 1,N)            M = N−I
  2   FORMAT (10F12.4)                  DO 10 J = 1,M
      STOP                              IF(A(J+1)−A(J))5,10,10
      END                          5   TEMP = A(J)
                                        A(J) = A(J+1)
                                        A(J+1) = TEMP
                                    10  CONTINUE
                                        RETURN
                                        END
```

NOTE: There is a specification statement missing from both of these programs of a type that is to be covered later.

4.152 The left side of frame 4.151 is the main program which reads the N numbers into the A array and calls in the ORDER routine to do the sorting, after which it prints out the sorted array. The program on the right is the SUBROUTINE which does the sorting, using the method of comparing adjacent numbers and swapping their position if they're out of the desired order. Admittedly the sort operation is only performed once in this example, but this is only a demonstration; in practice, a SUBROUTINE would only be used where its operation is required a number of times.

4.153 Notice that the example of frame 4.151 showed both the actual arguments and the dummy arguments with the same name. This was done to show that there is no harm in doing so, but the use of the same variable name is merely coincidental. The arguments in the SUBROUTINE are still dummies and are related to the variables of the same name in the main program only by virtue of their relative position in the argument list.

[true or false] The variable I as used in both programs in this example refers to a different quantity in each program. _____

true

4.154 Here are some check points in the writing and using of SUBROUTINE subprograms:

1. Choose a name that contains 1 to 6 alphanumeric characters and does not end in F.
2. Make certain that all the information needed in the SUBROUTINE is included in the arguments.
3. Make certain that all the information to be given to the calling program is also included.

4. Be sure that the SUBROUTINE has the required SUBROUTINE, RETURN, and END statements.
5. The program that calls upon the SUBROUTINE does so with a CALL statement.
6. The arguments in the calling program must agree in number and mode with the SUBROUTINE.

4.155   So far, then, this chapter has introduced you to five types of subprograms: library functions, built-in functions, arithmetic statement functions, FUNCTION subprograms, and SUBROUTINE subprograms. The built-in functions are available on all but the 705 systems; library functions are available for all but the 1620 system; arithmetic statement functions can be used with 705, 7070/7074, and 704/709/7090 systems. The FUNCTION and SUBROUTINE subprograms are available for the 7070/7074 and 704/709/7090 FORTRAN.

EXERCISE 4.8

Write a complete SUBROUTINE subprogram to invert an array; that is, place the first number of the first array at the end of the second array, the second number of the first array next to the end of the second array, etc. Use three arguments: the given array, the array into which the inverted array will be placed, and a fixed-point quantity which tells how long the arrays are. The SUBROUTINE is to be called INVERT.

4.156   You may have raised the question of how the computer understands which type of subprogram is called for. The process is one of elimination; the built-in functions have a distinct set of names, so if a function name is not one of this set it must either be defined in a function-defining statement or be treated as a library function. The FUNCTION is distinguished by a different type of name (no F), and, of course, the SUBROUTINE is called upon by the CALL statement. Incidentally, beware of naming a variable with the same name as a FUNCTION or SUBROUTINE used by the same program!

4.157   One last statement to be discussed in this manual is of the specification variety. This means that the statement does not tell the computer to *do* something, but rather gives the computer some information. The FORMAT statement is a specification statement, for example. The new statement is the DIMENSION statement.

4.158   The DIMENSION statement is used for specifying the size of arrays used in the program. The statement consists of the word DIMENSION followed by any number of array-size specifications separated by commas. (NOTE: learn well the spelling of the word DIMENSION, as the FORTRAN language accepts only the correct form!)

A DIMENSION statement must be used in all programs which contain
_____ .

4.159 The array-size specifications consist of the name of the array followed by a pair of parentheses containing a *constant* which defines the size of the array. For example, an array of 100 numbers called A would have an array-size specification of A(100).

The DIMENSION statement to specify the array described above would be
_____ .

4.160 If your program contains more than one array, you may specify all the arrays in a single DIMENSION statement or use more than one DIMENSION statement if you so choose. For example, a program containing three arrays called A, B, and C, each of which is 1000 numbers long, must have the statement DIMENSION A(1000),B(1000),C(1000) included in the program.

[true or false] The sequence of statements

> DIMENSION A(1000)
> DIMENSION B(1000)
> DIMENSION C(1000)

would be equivalent to the statement shown in the example above. _____

4.161 Every variable which is to be used with a subscript must appear in a DIMENSION statement. If this rule is not followed, the subscripted variable will look exactly like a FUNCTION name with argument. In fact, it will be treated as exactly that if its name is not listed in a DIMENSION.

[true or false] The statement DIMENSION A(10)B(20)C(30)D(40) is legitimate.
_____

4.162 Sometimes the size needed for an array will vary from run to run. In cases like these, an array size should be chosen that is large enough for the maximum size of array you will need. In no case should a subscript be allowed to exceed the size specified for the array in the DIMENSION statement.

The statement DIMENSION ARRAY(100), BLOCK(500) specifies array sizes of _____ and _____ .

4.163 When a dummy argument in a FUNCTION or SUBROUTINE is to be treated as an array (that is, it will be used with subscripts), the subprogram must *also* have a DIMENSION statement (in addition to the DIMENSION statement that must appear in the program that calls upon the subprogram).

[true or false] Any program that contains a subscripted variable must list that variable in a DIMENSION statement. _____

4.164 Repeat: a FUNCTION or SUBROUTINE that has a dummy argument which is an array *must* have a DIMENSION statement containing that name (even if the specified array size is *different* from that of the calling program) to permit subscripted use of the variable. Without this specification, the dummy array will be thought of as a FUNCTION by the subprogram, which would obviously be incorrect.

If a subprogram FUNCTION SUM(A,N) refers to a 10-number array A, the subprogram must contain the statement _____ .

4.165 Basically, then, the DIMENSION statement is used to give the computer some bookkeeping information. All variables that are used with subscripts must appear in a DIMENSION statement in the same program or subprogram; otherwise, the computer looks for a nonexistent FUNCTION subprogram and screeches to a halt.

The statement DIMENSION X(15),Y(10000), Z(50) specifies array sizes for the variables _____ , _____ , and _____ .

4.166 Important note: the DIMENSION statement must appear before any statements using the array names specified therein. Otherwise, the DIMENSION statement may be placed anywhere in the program (a slight exception is that the DIMENSION, like the FORMAT, cannot be the first or last statement in a DO-loop).

[true or false] The DIMENSION statement can be the last statement in the program. _____

EXERCISE 4.9

Write a program, including the DIMENSION statement, to read 100 numbers from cards (6 per card, 12 columns and 6 decimal places per number) into a block called ARRAY. Compute the square of each number, place in an array called SQUARE, and print the new array on the printer with the same FORMAT with which the original array was read.

4.167 FORTRAN permits a double-subscripting notation that is handy for referring to matrices and other groups having similar cross-reference notations. In this system, the variable name is followed by the open parenthesis, as usual, and followed in turn by two subscripts, separated by a comma, and a closing parenthesis.

[true or false] According to the above definition, $A(I,J)$ is a legitimate double-subscript notation. _____

true

4.168 The double-subscripted array is treated as a series of subarrays; the *first* subscript denotes the position referred to within the subarray and the *second* subscript refers to the particular subarray. Thus a 10×5 array called A is thought of as 5 blocks of 10 numbers each, and, for example, A(7,4) refers to the *seventh* number in the *fourth* block.

A 5×8 array would be thought of as being _____ blocks of _____ numbers in length.

eight, five

4.169 In order to use double-subscripting notation with a variable it must be specified in a special way; the DIMENSION statement for such a variable will have *two* constants in the array-size specification, the first of which denotes the subarray length, and the second of which specifies the number of subarrays.

[true or false] According to the above definition, the specification of a 10×5 array called A must be DIMENSION A(10,5). _____

true

4.170   Thus an array specified by DIMENSION A(10,5) is actually a 50-number array divided into 5 blocks of 10 numbers each. Double subscript form can be used only with variables that are double dimensioned as above, and a variable can be specified only one way or the other (for double *or* single subscripting).

A reference to the variable A as specified above such as A(8,3) refers to the _____ number in the _____ block of the array.

4.171   Any combination of double subscripts will refer to a unique position in the overall array; that is, there is no ambiguity that two different combinations might refer to the same quantity. The only limitation on the subscript values is that they cannot exceed their corresponding DIMENSION constant.

[true or false] With a specification of DIMENSION X(10,10), a reference to X(12,5) is legal. _____

4.172   The array-size specifications in the DIMENSION statement must be constants, fixing the array size when the program is written. The subscripts, however, may be variables or limited expressions, as in single subscript form, so long as their values are not permitted to exceed their corresponding DIMENSION specification.

With a specification of DIMENSION F(5,5), the reference of F(K,5) is legal as long as K does not exceed _____ .

4.173   The term "limited expression" in the preceding frame refers to the fact that either or both of the double subscripts may be in any one of the following forms: constant, variable, variable plus (or minus) a constant, constant times a variable, or constant times a variable plus (or minus) a constant.

[true or false] The above defined forms are the only ones permitted for single or double subscripts. _____

4.174   The examples in this frame represent *legitimate* uses of double-subscripting form:

A(1,1)	BLOCK(I,J)
X12(2*K,6)	ARRAY(N − 1,M − 1)
VALUE(K,5)	VECTOR(2 * K − 6,4 * K + 1)
NUMBER(1,INDEX)	LIST(5,4)

4.175 Regardless of whether a double subscript combination involves constants, variables, or "limited expressions" the resultant values of the subscripts will make reference to a particular quantity in the array. For example, with a specification of DIMENSION A(5,5) a reference to A(I,J) with values of 3 and 4 for I and J, respectively, will refer to the *third* number in the *fourth* block of the A array.

The A array as specified above contains a total of _____ numbers.

25

4.176 Double-subscript notation is very useful for such arrays as matrices. A matrix is nothing more than a group of numbers in rows and columns of a rectangular array. A 3×3 matrix is shown below in symbols:

$$
\begin{matrix}
a_{11} & a_{12} & a_{13} \\
a_{21} & a_{22} & a_{23} \\
a_{31} & a_{32} & a_{33}
\end{matrix}
$$

4.177 The matrix above uses double subscripts to denote row and column position in the matrix. For example, a_{23} is in the *second* row and *third* column. You can see that a matrix could be represented in FORTRAN notation with double subscripts in the same fashion.

An array A is a matrix; the reference to A(1,3) refers to the _____ row and the _____ column.

first, third

4.178 A rectangular array, then, can be expressed in a single array divided into groups of subarrays, where each subarray is a column (the first subscript is the row count). FORTRAN then becomes a useful tool for matrix handling, which in turn is a valuable tool for many mathematical problems.

A 6×8 matrix called AMATRX would be *specified* by the statement _____ .

DIMENSION AMATRX(6,8)

4.179 A doubly-subscripted array is actually laid out in single-array form in the following order (using a 3×4 array for illustration):

A(1,1) A(2,1) A(3,1)	A(1,2) A(2,2) A(3,2)
First column	Second column
A(1,3) A(2,3) A(3,3)	A(1,4) A(2,4) A(3,4)
Third column	Fourth column

The first number in each *column,* collected together, makes up a _____ of the matrix.

4.180   Since the computer must treat these two-dimensional arrays as single arrays partitioned into subarrays, it is important to understand how such an array is ordered. The list in the preceding frame shows this order, with the first subscript advancing more rapidly as the numbers in the list are counted off.

A double-subscripted reference to the fourth number in the sixth subarray (column) of a matrix called ARRAY would be _____ .

4.181   The 705, 7070/74, and 704/709/7090 versions of FORTRAN also permit a three-dimensional array notation. This is specified in a DIMENSION statement with three constants. The size of such an array is determined as in two-dimensional arrays, by the product of the DIMENSION constants; a $10 \times 10 \times 10$ array contains a total of 1000 numbers.

The statement DIMENSION A(6,5,4) specifies a _____-dimensional array.

4.182   Arrays which are specified in a DIMENSION statement as three-dimensional arrays are referred to in the program with triple-subscript form. The rules for such subscripts are the same as for two-dimensional arrays; the same form can be used for the subscripts themselves, and they are separated by commas.

[true or false] A reference such as ARRAY(I,J,K) is legal in three-dimensional arrays. _____

4.183   The three-dimensional array is treated by the computer as a single array divided into subarrays, each of which is a two-dimensional array subdivided as usual. For example, a $2 \times 3 \times 4$ array is a 24-number array consisting of *four* groups, each of which is a 2×3 array. Each 2×3 array is, of course, *three* groups of *two* numbers each.

The references A(1), B(1,1), and C(1,1,1) all refer to the _____ (first or last) quantity in the single array as treated by the computer.

4.184 The order of the equivalent single array of a three-dimensional array is determined by a similar rule to that of two-dimensional arrays. In counting off their positions, the first subscript is advanced most rapidly; each time it reaches its limit, the second subscript is advanced; each time the second subscript reaches its limit, the third subscript is advanced. An example showing this occurs in the next frame.

In a $4 \times 5 \times 6$ array, the reference A(4,5,6) refers to the [first or last] _____ number in the array.

last

4.185 The following list is the order (in single array form) of a three-dimensional array, $2 \times 3 \times 4$, using symbols:

A(1, 1, 1)	A(2, 1, 1)	A(1, 2, 1)	A(2, 2, 1)	A(1, 3, 1)	A(2, 3, 1)
A(1, 1, 2)	A(2, 1, 2)	A(1, 2, 2)	A(2, 2, 2)	A(1, 3, 2)	A(2, 3, 2)
A(1, 1, 3)	A(2, 1, 3)	A(1, 2, 3)	A(2, 2, 3)	A(1, 3, 3,)	A(2, 3, 3)
A(1, 1, 4)	A(2, 1, 4)	A(1, 2, 4)	A(2, 2, 4)	A(1, 3, 4)	A(2, 3, 4)

4.186 The multiple-subscripting form extends to self-indexed lists for input and output statements also. The double-subscript notation used with self-indexed lists permits two index definitions acting like nested DO-loops. This is denoted with parentheses within parentheses, each pair containing an index definition.

4.187 An input or output statement may have two-dimensional arrays in its list. The self-indexing form then contains two index definitions. The format of this notation is: *two* open parentheses, the variable name, two dummy subscripts (variables) in parentheses, a comma, and an index definition for *one* of the dummy subscripts, followed by a closing parenthesis balancing the innermost of the left-side open parentheses. Then comes a comma and a second index definition for the other dummy subscript, followed by the last parenthesis.

[true or false] According to the above definition, the statement READ 1, ((A(I,J), I = 1, 10), J = 1, 20) is a legal example of two-dimensional self-indexing form. _____

true

4.188 The foregoing example, READ 1,((A(I,J), I = 1, 10), J = 1, 20), demonstrates the list which will read in a two-dimensional array called A. As pointed out before, this double indexing behaves like nested DO-loops, such that I in this example is cycled from 1 to 10, then J is stepped by 1 before I cycles again.

The dummy subscripts in the example shown above are _____ and _____ .

I, J

4.189   The statement READ 1, ((A(I,J), I = 1, 10), J = 1, 20) will read 200 quantities into the A array in the following order: A(1, 1), A(2, 1), A(3, 1), . . . , A(10, 1), A(1, 2), A(2, 2), A(3, 2), . . . , A(10, 20). In other words, the innermost index definition corresponds to the innermost DO-loop, cycling most rapidly.

The 31st quantity read by the statement shown above will be placed in A(_____ , _____).

4.190   As the example READ 1, ((A(I,J), I = 1, 10), J = 1, 20) has demonstrated, the double-subscripted version of self-indexed lists is nothing more than an ordinary self-indexed sequence (inner parentheses) which cycles normally and repeats its complete cycle according to the control of the second index definition (outer parentheses). For every combination of index values a specific reference is made to the indicated array.

[true or false] The outer parentheses enclosing the second index definition must also enclose the entire self-indexed sequence. _____

4.191   Failure to place a comma where it is required is the source of a great deal of grief for FORTRAN programmers. A statement such as READ 1, ((A(I,J), I = 1, 10), J = 1, 20) has *six* commas, and every one of them is absolutely required! Note their position, and be sure that you include them, not only for this type of statement, but for all statements which require commas.

Punctuate the statement: PRINT 100((A(JK)J = 1 5)K = 1 8)

4.192   While it seems perfectly natural to read double-subscripted arrays by cycling the first subscript most rapidly in the self-indexed notation, it is perfectly permissible to reverse the index definitions, as follows: READ 1, ((A(I,J), J = 1, 20), I = 1, 10) which will read A(1, 1), A(1, 2), A(1, 3), etc. in that order.

Reversing the index definitions from the previous example, the _____ (first or second) subscript varies most rapidly in the index cycling.

4.193   Two-dimensional arrays that are matrices are often read by a statement such as READ 1, ((A(I,J,), J = 1, 20), I = 1, 10) so that the numbers can be punched on the cards in *row* order rather than *column* order. Remember this statement reads in the order A(1, 1), A(1, 2), A(1, 3), etc., which corresponds to the row designation.

The "normal" order of A(1, 1), A(2, 1), A(3, 1), etc., corresponds to _____ [row or column] order for matrices.

column

4.194   Any two-dimensional array that is thought of in terms of rows and columns should certainly be *printed* in rows of numbers that represent the rows of the matrix or whatever. The backward indexing scheme just illustrated for reading is usually applied to printing (or print images) for this reason.

Write a statement to PRINT the matrix A using I and J for dummy subscripts, printing the 10 $\times$ 10 array row-wise. _____

PRINT 1, ((A(I,J), J = 1, 10), I = 1, 10)

4.195   Like the single self-indexed list with one index, the double indexed form can be used with more than one variable. For example, READ 1, ((X(I,J), Y(I,J), I = 1, 10), J = 1, 100) will read a pair of numbers for each combination of indices, cycling them in the usual fashion.

The third number read with the above statement will be placed in _____(_____, _____).

X(2, 1)
  The first number goes in X(1, 1), the second in Y(1, 1).

4.196   Any input or output statement can have more than one self-indexed list (single or double indexed) in a single statement along with single variables, if desired. For example, a list can become as complicated as PRINT 1, M, N, (A(I), I = 1, M), ((B(I,J), I = 1, M), J = 1, N), which contains two single variables and single and double indexed lists.

The third value printed with the above statement is (name) _____.

A(1)

4.197   So far, then, you have seen examples of double-subscript notation, which can be used with any variable appearing in a DIMENSION statement in two-dimensional form, used in arithmetic expressions and in input and output statements. The latter application requires two index definitions for the two dummy subscripts in the list, with two sets of parentheses setting off the inner and outer definitions. These double index specifications then behave like nested DO-loops, cycling the inner index for each value of the outer.

Write a statement to read from tape 8 according to FORMAT number 15, reading first a 20×20 array called BLOCK and *then* a 10×50 array called ARRAY, reading the former in row order (second subscript cycled most rapidly) and the latter in column order. Use I and J for the subscript-index variables.

> READ INPUT TAPE 8, 15, ((BLOCK(I,J), J = 1, 20), I = 1, 20) ((ARRAY (I,J), I = 1, 10), J = 1, 50)
>
> If your answer agrees exactly with the one shown (all thirteen commas and twelve parentheses required) you may skip to Exercise 4.10 on page 187. If your answer was incorrect, continue with the next frame.

4.198 The problem was to read from tape 8 with FORMAT number 15, so the first part of the statement poses no difficulty: READ INPUT TAPE 8, 15, . . . ; the real test is in constructing the two double indexed lists correctly. The first array, named BLOCK, is 20×20 in size and is to be read *row-wise,* meaning that the *second* dummy index is cycled by the *inner* index definition, as in ((BLOCK(I,J), J = 1, 20), I = 1, 20).

The third number read with the list shown above will become the value of BLOCK(_____ , _____).

1, 3

4.199 The second array, named ARRAY, is 10×50 in size and is to be read *column-wise,* meaning that its first dummy subscript is to be cycled with the inner index definition (most rapidly). Thus, a double indexed list for this array looks like ((ARRAY(I,J), I = 1, 10), J = 1, 50). Since the problem stated that you were to read the first array completely and then read the second array, the two separate double indexed lists appear in sequence in the input statement.

The third number read with the list shown above will become the value of ARRAY(_____ , _____).

3, 1

4.200 Try a similar problem. Write a statement to write on tape 5 using FORMAT number 1010, writing the AMATRX array, of dimension 30×50, row-wise, followed by the values of the variables X and Y. Use dummy subscripts I and J as before. _____

EXERCISE 4.10

Given ten cards, each of which contains a row of a 10×10 matrix (10F7.1 in the FORMAT), write the necessary DIMENSION, READ, and FORMAT statements to place the matrix in the array called BLOCK.

That concludes the new material about the FORTRAN language covered in this manual. The next several frames illustrate the ways of preparing a written program for actual execution on the computer. Naturally every system cannot be covered in detail, but the general concepts will be covered, and most computing centers will be glad to furnish details and rules concerning their handling of FORTRAN programs.

4.201 All FORTRAN programs are written in basically the same language, but most computers are programmed in numerical codes peculiar to a particular system. Consequently, each computer system must have its own means of translating a FORTRAN program into its own code system. For example, a 704 (or 709 or 7090) must translate the statement $Y = A + B(I)$ into three numeric codes which might look like:

$$050000000101$$
$$030200100152$$
$$060100000100$$

4.202 Fortunately, a program already exists for all these computers which will do this translation from the FORTRAN language into the computer's instruction code. This program is called the *FORTRAN compiler* and it reads a FORTRAN program as its input and produces a computer-coded program as output.

The program which translates programs from FORTRAN language into computer code is called a _____ _____ .

4.203 Once a program is written in FORTRAN language, the process of executing the program on the computer becomes a two-stage process: translating from FORTRAN to computer code and running the computer-coded version to get the answers.

[true or false] Before the program can be executed on a computer, it must first be translated into the computer's own code. _____

true

4.204   Every computer equipped to handle FORTRAN programs, then, must have its own *compiler* which will read your FORTRAN program and produce for you a program ready to execute on that computer (or a similar computer).

The input to the FORTRAN compiler is a _____ _____ .

FORTRAN program.

4.205   Obviously there must be some way to transcribe your FORTRAN program into a form that the compiler can read. This is usually done by punching the statements on cards with an 026 key-punch machine. FORTRAN statements are punched one statement per card (some systems permit more than one card per statement) with a card layout as shown in the next frame.

4.206

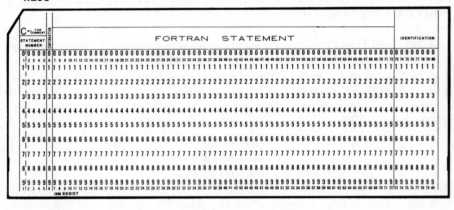

4.207   In the type of card layout above, a statement number, if any, is punched in columns 1 through 5 of the card, and the statement itself is punched anywhere in columns 7 through 72. As long as the statement appears in the proper field (columns 7 to 72) there is no restriction as to which columns are used for any part of the statement. This means that blank columns (unpunched) are ignored, and only the sequence that is actually punched is read. This is possible because of FORTRAN's liberal use of punctuation to set off parts of statements for the compiler.

4.208   The next two frames show the same FORTRAN statement punched in two different ways, both of which are equivalent as far as the translating program is concerned. Notice that blanks are used at will, pointing out the fact that they are not counted as part of the statement.

4.209

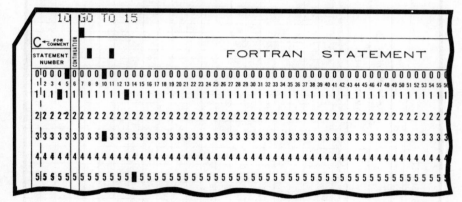

4.210

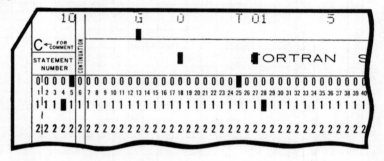

This is admittedly ridiculous, but demonstrates that the statement can be spaced in any desired manner. This card is perfectly legal as a representation of the statement GO TO 15.

4.211   A FORTRAN program must be punched statement by statement into cards in the format shown on the preceding frames. It often helps to have written the program on a coding sheet which is blocked off like the card layout (see following frame).

4.212   A typical FORTRAN coding sheet is shown on page 190.

4.213   The only time that blank or unpunched columns are counted by the compiler as being significant is when they are included in an H field in a FORMAT statement. You will remember that this is the way of writing alphanumeric infor-

IBM DATA SYSTEMS DIVISION
DEVELOPMENT LABORATORIES

SYMBOLIC AND FORTRAN CODING SHEET   7090

NAME _____   DEPT. ___   PROBLEM NO. ___   PHONE NO. ___   DATE DUE OUT ___   SHEET ___ OF ___   PROGRAM TITLE: ___

PUNCH 73-80

☐ YES ☐ NO

FORTRAN CHECK ☐

SYMBOLIC CHECK ☐

STATEMENT NUMBER	CONT	SYMBOL	OPERATION	FORTRAN STATEMENT → ADDRESS, TAG, DECREMENT / COUNT →	IDENT.	PG.	LINE
1 2 3 4 5	6	7 8 9 10 11 12	13 14 15 16 17 18 19 20 21 22 23 24 25 26 27 28 29 30 31 32 33 34 35 36 37 38 39 40 41 42 43 44 45 46 47 48 49 50 51 52 53 54 55 56 57 58 59 60 61 62 63 64 65 66 67 68 69 70 71 72		73 74 75 76	77 78	79 80
							0 1 0
							0 2 0
							0 3 0
							0 4 0
							0 5 0
							0 6 0
							0 7 0
							0 8 0
							0 9 0
							1 0 0
							1 1 0
							1 2 0
							1 3 0
							1 4 0
							1 5 0
							1 6 0
							1 7 0
							1 8 0
							1 9 0
							2 0 0
							2 1 0

mation, and the blank is a legal character in this set. A statement such as
1 FORMAT (19H*b*THIS*b*IS*b*THE*b*OUTPUT) might be punched on a card as
shown on the following frame.

4.214

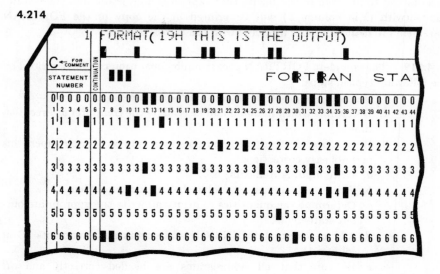

4.215 Statements which are too long to fit in a single card can in some systems such as the 704/709/7090 FORTRAN be continued on up to nine *additional* cards by placing a nonzero punch in column 6 of the card for each card which is a continuation of the preceding card (that is, the *first* card in such a series does *not* have such a punch). The following frame demonstrates this characteristic.

4.216

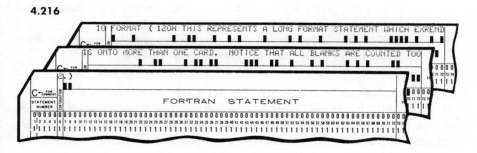

4.217 The preceding frame shows a FORMAT statement with an H field so long that it requires three cards to contain the entire statement. Notice that the first card is a normal card (no continuation punch in column 6), but the next two have 1 and 2 respectively in this column, meaning that they are continuations of the statement beginning on the first card. The character chosen for the continuation mark is arbitrary; often the integers 1 to 9 are used to indicate the order. The effect of this punch is to create an equivalent card image that places columns 7 to 72 of the continuation card immediately after column 72 of the preceding one.

4.218 Any FORTRAN statement that has the letter C punched in column 1—normally reserved for statement numbers—will not be included in the translated program. In fact, this card can contain any sequence of punches you desire. This permits you to intersperse comments that explain the program, and these statements (with C in column 1) will be printed in the copy of the FORTRAN statements that the compiler produces with the translation.

4.219 The complete FORTRAN programming operation can be described by the following typical steps:
1. Organize the problem, determining equations used, etc.
2. Determine which items should be read by the computer at execution time.
3. Write a first draft of the program statements on scratch paper (this permits easy corrections).
   a. Write input statements.
   b. Write the statements to solve the particular problem.
   c. Determine the quantities to print and write the appropriate output statements.
   d. Add necessary DIMENSION statements and comments (C in column 1).
   e. Be sure that all subprograms are headed correctly and *all* programs have END statements.
4. Copy final draft on coding sheets.
5. Punch the program on cards (many computing centers offer this service if coding forms are used).
6. Using the FORTRAN compiler program, translate your program to a computer-coded one.
7. Execute your computer-coded program, with any input data you are reading, and obtain answers.
8. Examine the results and verify them, debugging if necessary (correct the FORTRAN statements and repeat at step 6).

This concludes this course in basic FORTRAN. As if your head were not spinning enough already, you must understand that this manual has covered only the elementary features of the language, along with a few common tricks of programming with FORTRAN. Many systems also provide advanced features such as boolean algebra statements, complex arithmetic, double-precision arithmetic, special debugging aids, monitoring of the job execution, etc. It is hoped that this course has given you sufficient background to understand the language (our main objective) and, with experience, to make use of it properly.

The following pages contain the examination for this chapter, and following this test and the solutions to applied problems are two possible exercises to be actually run on a computer if it is available. The first of those two exercises is of the scientific computing nature, while the second is oriented to data-processing techniques.

PART 4: EXAMINATION

1. Write a single arithmetic statement function definition for the following formulas:

Name	Formula	Arguments
CUBRTF	cube root $= x^{(.333333)}$	X
SIN2XF	$\sin(2x) = 2\sin(x)\cos(x)$	X
ROOTF	root $= \dfrac{-b + \sqrt{b^2 - 4ac}}{2a}$	A,B,C
LOG10F	$\log_{10} x = 0.43429448 \log_e x$	X
FLOORF	$f(x) = \begin{cases} x^2 & \text{if } x > 6.0 \\ 36.0 & \text{if } x \leq 6.0 \end{cases}$	X

CUBRTF(X) = _____

SIN2XF(X) = _____

ROOTF(A, B, C) = _____

LOG10F(X) = _____

FLOORF(X) = _____

2. Given an array of positive numbers, 500 in all, called LIST (fixed-point), compute the *square* root of each value which is an *even* number or the *fourth* root of each value which is an *odd* number. Place the results in the floating-point array called ARRAY in the same order that the original values were found in LIST. Include an appropriate DIMENSION statement.

3. Indicate by listing subscripts the order of the lists in the following DIMENSION statements. For example, DIMENSION A(2, 2) would result in the order: (1, 1), (2, 1), (1, 2), (2, 2)

DIMENSION X(5, 4) ____ ____ ____ ____ ____ ____ ____ ____

____ ____ ____ ____ ____ ____ ____ ____

DIMENSION ARRAY(2, 5) ____ ____ ____ ____ ____ ____ ____

____ ____

DIMENSION QUOTA(2, 2, 2) ____ ____ ____ ____ ____ ____ ____

____

4. Write a FUNCTION subprogram called G with two arguments X and A. The FUNCTION is to be programmed to give the value ax^2 if x is less than zero or the value ax^3 if x is equal to or greater than zero.

5. Write a SUBROUTINE subprogram called MATMPY which will multiply two matrices, each of which is 10×10 in size, having as arguments A, B, and C, where A and B are the matrices to be multiplied and C is the product matrix. Remember, the argument variables are arrays (must appear in DIMENSION statement) and they are listed in the SUBROUTINE statement by name only (without any subscripts). In general, the product of two matrices is formed by multiplying each number in a row by a number in a column and adding

the products, repeating for all combinations of rows and columns. In formula form it is (for all combinations of i and j)

$$c_{ij} = \sum_{k=1}^{10} (a_{ik})\,(b_{kj})$$

or, for example:

$$c_{11} = a_{11}b_{11} + a_{12}b_{21} + a_{13}b_{31} + a_{14}b_{41} + \ldots + a_{1,\,10}b_{10,\,1}$$
$$c_{21} = a_{21}b_{11} + a_{22}b_{21} + a_{23}b_{31} + a_{24}b_{41} + \ldots + a_{2,\,10}b_{10,\,1}$$
$$\ldots\ldots\ldots\ldots\ldots\ldots\ldots\ldots\ldots\ldots\ldots\ldots\ldots\ldots\ldots\ldots$$

$$c_{10,\,1} = a_{10,\,1}b_{11} + a_{10,\,2}b_{21} + a_{10,\,3}b_{31} + \ldots + a_{10,\,10}b_{10,\,1}$$
$$c_{12} = a_{11}b_{12} + a_{12}b_{22} + a_{13}b_{32} + a_{14}b_{42} + \ldots + a_{1,\,10}b_{10,\,2}$$

In other words, any ijth element of the c matrix is composed of ten products added together, the products being corresponding elements of the ith row of the a matrix and the jth column of the b matrix multiplied together. Notice that the examples above show that the first subscript of the a matrix always agrees with the first subscript of the desired c element, while the second subscript of the b matrix always agrees with the second subscript of the c element. The column subscript of a and the row subscript of b are also always the same. Thus, this problem can be handled with three nested DO-loops, the innermost of which controls the summation.

6. Write a program that uses the FUNCTION of problem 4 and the SUBROUTINE of problem 5 in the following manner:

   (a) Read from cards a 10×10 array called BLOCK, reading column-wise (first subscript cycled most rapidly), reading six numbers per card and four decimal places.

   (b) Read from tape 2 a 10×10 array called BMATRX, reading row-wise (second subscript cycled most rapidly), with the same card image FORMAT.

   (c) Call on MATMPY to multiply the two matrices, giving BLOCK as the first argument (premultiplier) and BMATRX as the second (postmultiplier), and place the result in an array called ARRAY.

   (d) For each element of ARRAY, compute the value of G(D,ARRAY(I,J)) using the FUNCTION of problem 4, with D having a value of 5.0, and replace the original value of ARRAY with the one computed with the FUNCTION.

   (e) Print on the attached printing device the entire ARRAY contents (row-wise), ten numbers per line with four decimal places.

SOLUTIONS TO EXERCISES

Part 1

1.1 (a) X + Y − Z
(b) A * X + B * Y + C * Z
(c) A/B + C/D
(d) A + 2 * B + 3 * C + 4 * D + 5 * C/2

1.2 (a) A, B   (c) X, Y
(b) C, 2   (d) X, 3

1.3 (a) A, B   (c) Y, Z
(b) X, Y   (d) D, 2

1.4 (a) floating   (e) fixed   (h) floating
(b) floating   (f) fixed   (i) floating
(c) fixed   (g) fixed   (j) fixed
(d) floating

1.5 (a) floating   (c) floating   (e) fixed
(b) mixed   (d) mixed

1.6 (a) F = XM * A
(b) V = 4./3. * 3.1415926 * R ** 3
(c) Y = A * X ** 2 + B * X + C
(d) S = S0 + V0 * T + 0.5 * G * T ** 2

1.7 (a) +   (c) +   (e) −
(b) −   (d) +

Part 2

2.1   IF (A − 25.0)30,1,30
1 IF (B − 25.0)30,2,30
2 IF (C − 25.0)30,3,30
3 IF (D − 25.0)30,15,30

2.2   IF (X − Y)1,1,2
2 IF (X − Z)30,10,10
1 IF (X − Z)40,20,20

2.3   I = 0
10 I = I + 1
INDEX (I) = I
IF (I − 2000)10,20,20
20 (continue on in program)

2.4   SMALLX = X(1)
DO 40 I = 2, 100
IF (X(I))10,20,20
10 X(I) = −X(I)
20 IF (X(I) − SMALLX)30,40,40
30 SMALLX = X(I)
40 CONTINUE

2.5
```
      DO 10 I = 1,1000
      J = 1001 - I
   10 B(J) = A(I)
```

2.6
```
      N = 0
      DO 100 I = 1,1000
      IF (A(I) - 10.0)100,100,50
   50 N = N + 1
  100 CONTINUE
```

2.7
```
      K = 0
      DO 10 I = 1,20
      DO 10 J = 1,20
      K = K + 1
   10 C(K) = A(I) * B(J)
```

2.8
```
      SUM = 0.0
      DO 100 I = 1,10000
      IF (SENSE SWITCH 1)10,20
   10 B(I) = A(I)
      GO TO 100
   20 C(I) = A(I)
  100 SUM = SUM + A(I)
```

2.9
```
DO 1 I = 1,10
GO TO (10,20,30,40,50,60,70,80,90,100),I
```

2.10
```
      DO 100 I = 1,1500
      C(I) = A(I)/B(I)
      IF QUOTIENT OVERFLOW 10,20
   10 PAUSE 1
      GO TO 100
   20 IF DIVIDE CHECK 30,100
   30 PAUSE 2
  100 CONTINUE
```

Part 3

3.1
```
      READ 1,A,B,C,D,E,F,G,H,O,P
```

3.2
```
      DO 10 I = 1,100
   10 READ 1, A(I), B(I), C(I)
```

3.3
```
      READ 1,(X(I), I = 1, 100),(Y(I), I = 1, 100)
```

3.4
```
      DO 10 I = 1, 500
   10 READ 1,N,(W(N),X(N),Y(N),Z(N))
```

3.5
```
      READ INPUT TAPE 16,1,(K(I),I = 1,99,2)
```

3.6
```
      (a)   FORMAT (F8.1)
      (b)   FORMAT (F10.8)
      (c)   FORMAT (F6.2)
      (d)   FORMAT (F7.0)
      (e)   FORMAT (F2.1)
```

3.7
```
      FORMAT (F10.5,F8.3,F12.0)
```

3.8
```
    1 FORMAT (5F14.3)
```

3.9   READ 1,(X(I),I = 11,20)
   1   FORMAT (10F7.4)

3.10   READ INPUT TAPE 20,1,(JOE(I),JIM(I),ANDY(I),BOB(I),
                                                           FRANK(I),I = 1,100)
   1   FORMAT(2I5, 3F10.3)

3.11

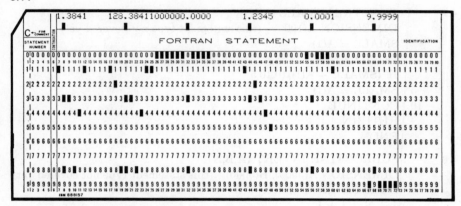

3.12   READ 1,(X(I),I = 1,1000)
        READ INPUT TAPE 9,1,(X(I),I = 1001,2500)
   1   FORMAT (8F9.3)

3.13   PRINT 1,(A(I),B(I),C(I),I = 1, 100)
   1   FORMAT (3F20.4)

3.14   DO 10 J = 1, 100
        READ INPUT TAPE 11,1,(A(I),I = 1,10)
  10 WRITE OUTPUT TAPE 12,1,(A(I),I = 1,10)
   1   FORMAT (10F7.3)

3.15   PRINT 1,(ANSWER(I),I = 1,10)
   1   FORMAT (23H*b*FINAL*b*COMPUTED*b*RESULTS//(F20.2))

Part 4

4.1   DO 10 I = 1, 100
        X = ANGLE(I)/57.29578
  10 Y(I) = ATANF (SINF(X) ** 2) + ((SINF(X)/COSF(X)) ** 3)

4.2   (*a*) fixed   (*c*) floating   (*e*) fixed
       (*b*) floating   (*d*) floating

4.3   IF (ABSF(X) − .001)100,100,10

4.4   Y = MAX1F(X,5.0) ** 2 or Y = MAX1F(X ** 2,25.0)

4.5   Four possible solutions:
A = MIN0F (XMAX0F(I1,I2,I3,I4), XMAX0F (J1,J2,J3,J4))
A = MIN1F (MAX0F (I1,I2,I3,I4), MAX0F (J1,J2,J3,J4))
A = XMIN0F (same argument as first solution above)
A = XMIN1F (same argument as second solution above)

4.6   ANGLEF(X,Y) = ATANF (X/Y)

4.7   FUNCTION SMALL (A,N)
DIMENSION A(1000)   (this statement type not covered yet)
SMALL = A(1)
DO 10 I = 2,N
IF (SMALL − A(I))10,10,5
  5 SMALL = A(I)
10 CONTINUE
RETURN
END

4.8   SUBROUTINE INVERT (A,B,N)
DIMENSION A(5000), B(5000)   (this statement type not covered yet)
DO 10 I = 1,N
J = N − I + 1
10 B(J) = A(I)
RETURN
END

4.9   DIMENSION ARRAY (100), SQUARE (100)
READ 1, (ARRAY(I), I = 1, 100)
  1 FORMAT (6F12.6)
DO 10 I = 1, 100
10 SQUARE(I) = ARRAY(I) ** 2
PRINT 1, (SQUARE(I), I = 1, 100)
STOP
END

4.10   DIMENSION BLOCK(10,10)
READ 1, ((BLOCK(I,J), J = 1, 10), I = 1, 10)
  1 FORMAT (10F7.1)

FINAL EXAMINATION

Problem 1

I. Write a set of programs to do the following:
   A. Main program
      1. Read (tape 5) an integer to be used as an index limit.*
      2. Read (tape 5) up to ten floating-point numbers, the amount to be determined by the integer previously read.*
      3. Read (tape 5) a single floating-point number to be used as a starting point ("first guess" as explained below).*
      4. Using the numbers read in (2) as coefficients of a polynomial in *x,* call a subroutine to compute the coefficients of the first derivative of the polynomial. (See *B* below.)
      5. Using the function described in C below, compute the values of the polynomial and its derivative for the "first guess" value of *x* read in (3) above.
      6. Using the Newton-Raphson iteration method (explained below) compute the root of the polynomial nearest to the initial guess.
      7. Write (tape 6) all the input information and the computed root, suitably labeled.*
      8. Go back to beginning and read more data (instead of STOP) for solution of another polynomial (program will stop when data runs out).
   B. SUBROUTINE DIFFER (A, B, N)
      Using a subroutine similar to the title above, compute the coefficients of the first derivative of the polynomial, given the A array as the polynomial coefficients and placing the derivative coefficients in the B array for use in the main program.
      Consider an *n*th degree polynomial in general form as:

      $$a_1 + a_2x + a_3x^2 + \ldots + a_{n+1}x^n$$

      The first coefficient read in your main program is a_1; the second, a_2; etc. The derivative, in general, is

      $$(a_2) + (2a_3)x + (3a_4)x^2 + \ldots + (na_{n+1})x^{n-1}$$

      The coefficients (in parentheses above) are to be computed in this subroutine (B array). *Don't Forget* DIMENSION *Statement!*
   C. FUNCTION SOLVE (A, X, N)
      Using a function subprogram similar to the title shown above, compute a general polynomial value, given an array A and the value X. This function can be used in computing both the polynomial value and the derivative value for each iteration as explained below.

   * Standard input and output tape numbers vary; check at the computer where this program will be run.

199

II. Theory. The Newton-Raphson method requires that an initial "guess" of the root is provided. The value of the polynomial and the value of its derivative are computed using this value.

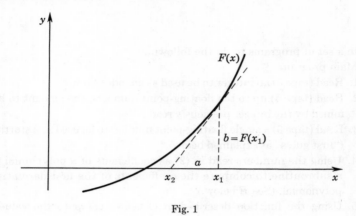

Fig. 1

In Figure 1, b is the value of the polynomial at x_1, and the slope of the line tangent to the curve is the value of the derivative of the polynomial at x_1. Hence,

$$\frac{b}{a} = \frac{F(x_1)}{a} = F'(x_1) \qquad \text{value of the derivative at } x_1$$

Rearranging terms:

$$a = \frac{F(x_1)}{F'(x_1)}$$

and

$$x_1 = x_2 + a$$

so that

$$x_2 = x_1 - a = x_1 - \frac{F(x_1)}{F'(x_1)}$$

The Newton-Raphson iteration method simply solves the formula

$$x_{i+1} = x_i - \frac{F(x_i)}{F'(x_i)}$$

a sufficient number of times to "converge" on a solution. Each computed x value is substituted back into the right-hand side of the above formula to produce a new x value. This "iterating" process is demonstrated below.

If x_1 were the "first guess" of the actual root value, the first computation of the formula shown above will produce x_2; repeating, using x_2, the formula computes x_3. This process repeats until the latest x is within a prescribed allowable "error amount" of the actual root.

This iteration method, under certain conditions, may be unstable; that is, it might proceed away from the root (diverge) or not move at all (oscillate). The samples used in this problem will all converge (obtain a root).

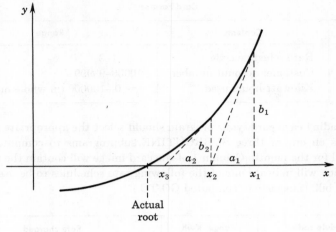

Actual
root

Fig. 2

To use this method in a program solve the polynomial and its derivative for the "initial guess" value which was read in. Compute the correction term, $F(x_1)/F'(x_1)$, and subtract from x_1, *replacing* x_1 with this value. Recompute the polynomial and derivative and obtain a new x. Check each time to see if the absolute value of the correction term is less than the error limit (0.000005 for this problem). When this point has been reached, the last computed x is the root approximation good to four decimal places.

III. Procedure
    A. Write main program, subroutine, and function.
    B. Punch programs.
    C. Punch data in cards (to be placed on tape 5) for the following polynomials.
      1. $2x^4 + x^3 - 9x^2 - x - 6.6498$ ("guess" = 2.0)
      2. $x^2 - 1.14159x - 6.28318$ ("guess" = 6.0)
      3. $x^9 - x^8 + x^7 - x^6 + x^5 - x^4 - x^3 + 2x^2 - x + 0.5$ ("guess" = 3.0)

      Polynomial roots:
      1.   2.10579
      2.   3.14159
      3.   −0.94011

Problem 2

Suppose that an electric power company has collected its monthly meter readings, punched them on cards in the format shown below, and placed these card images on tape. Write a program to read each card image, one by one, from tape unit 5 and write on tape 6 all the card information plus the customer's charge.*

* Standard input and output tape numbers vary; check at the computer where this program will be run.

Column	Contents	Range
1	Rate schedule code	1–3
11–15	Customer account number	10000–99999
25–30	Kilowatt-hours used	0.–100000 (in whole numbers)

After reading each card, your program should select the appropriate statement which calls on one of three SUBROUTINE subprograms to compute the customer's bill for the month. Column 1 of the card image will contain the number 1, 2, or 3 which will indicate one of the following rate schedules to be used in computing the bill. (Suggestion: computed GO TO.)

Schedule code	Range, Kwh	Rate charged
1 + (normal house power)	50 or less	$3.00 (minimum bill)
	51–150	$3.00 plus $0.045/kwh over 50
	151–250	$7.50 plus $0.035/kwh over 150
	over 250	$11.00 plus $0.03/kwh over 250
2 (house plus hot water and/or heat)	150 or less	$7.50 (minimum bill)
	151–350	$7.50 plus $0.03/kwh over 150
	Over 350	$13.50 plus $.025/kwh over 350
3 (industrial rate)	1000 or less	$30.00 (minimum bill)
	1001–5000	$30.00 plus $0.02/kwh over 1000
	5001–20000	$110.00 plus $.015/kwh over 5000
	Over 20000	$335.00 plus $.01/kwh over 20000

After the SUBROUTINE has computed the monthly bill your program should write this information on tape 6 as described above in the following format:*

Column	Contents
1	Blank (carriage control)
3	Rate schedule code value
24–28	Account number value
42–48	Number of kilowatt-hours used
60–66	Computed bill (dollars with two decimal places)

One line in the preceding format should be written for every card image read. After the tape image is written, your program should return to the statement which reads the next card (GO TO . . .), thus providing a loop with no exit control

* Standard input and output tape numbers vary; check at the computer where this program will be run.

(no DO or IF statements), since the computer will stop when the tape is empty of card images.

Just before reading the first of the card images on tape 5 your program should write a single line image on tape 6 for page titling purposes. This line should be laid out as follows (items in quotes to be copied directly):*

Column	Contents
1	1 (carriage-control)
2–5	RATE
22–30	ACCT. NO.
41–50	UNITS USED
61–66	CHARGE

The problem, then, is to write a main program that performs the following:
1. Title the page (line image on tape 6).*
2. Read a card image on tape 5 containing schedule code, account number, and units used.*
3. Call upon the appropriate SUBROUTINE to compute the billing charge.
4. Write a line image containing the input information plus the bill charge.
5. Go back to read a new card image (but do not retitle the page).

Along with the main program you must write three SUBROUTINE subprograms (suggested names: HOUSE, HEAT, and FACTRY), each of which computes the bill for a particular rate schedule. Two argument quantities seem adequate (amount of energy used and computed bill). Don't forget the required RETURN and END statements for *each* subprogram (the job can be done with one SUBROUTINE if you wish).

The following are suggested card images to test your program. With each is given the correct billing charge to verify your output.

Rate code	Account number	Kilowatt-hours used	(Correct bill)
1	12345	176	$ 8.41
3	55555	24590	380.90
1	98765	40	3.00
2	34567	151	7.53
3	43234	20000	335.00
2	56565	454	16.10
1	54321	980	32.90
3	22222	1501	40.02
2	69696	75	7.50
3	12321	856	30.00

* Standard input and output tape numbers vary; check at the computer where this program will be run.

INDEX

Prepared by Frank A. Yett, chairman, Department of Computer Sciences, and Carol Thrun, laboratory assistant, Computing Center, Pasadena City College, Pasadena, California.

Index numbers refer to frames rather than pages.